DINERS

KAREN OFFITZER

MetroBooks

MetroBooks

An Imprint of Friedman/Fairfax Publishers

Published in 1997 by Michael Friedman Publishing Group, Inc.
by arrangement with Todtri Productions Limited.

Copyright © 1997 by Todtri Productions Limited.

Library of Congress Cataloging-in-Publication Data available on request.

ISBN 1-56799-604-3

This book was designed and produced by Todtri Productions Limited,
P.O. Box 572, New York, NY 10116-0572 FAX: (212) 695-6988

Author: Karen Offitzer

Publisher: Robert M. Tod
Editorial Director: Elizabeth Loonan
Senior Editor: Cynthia Sternau
Project Editor: Ann Kirby
Photo Editor: Meiers Tambeau
Production Coordinator: Jay Weiser
Designer: Jacquerie Productions

Printed and bound in Singapore

For bulk purchases and special sales, please contact:
Friedman/Fairfax Publishers
Attention: Sales Department
15 West 26th Street
New York, NY 10010
212/685-6610 FAX 212/685-1307

Visit our website:
http://www.metrobooks.com

PHOTO CREDITS

H. Armstrong Roberts
Becker / Zefa 72 (top)
Ralph Drubner 76
R. Kord 39 (bottom), 100 (top)

The Art Institute of Chicago 62

John Baeder 5, 13, 18–19, 32–33, 37, 41, 73, 79, 98–99 (left),
101, 105 (right)

Scott Barrow 12 (bottom), 36, 55

Robert W. Bone 74

Paula Borchardt 89

Rudi Von Briel 7 (top), 88, 91

Corbis-Bettmann 11, 16, 32 (bottom left), 42, 43, 48–49, 50, 52,
53, 61, 82, 99 (right), 100 (bottom), 107, 118, 122 (top)

Culver Pictures 14, 28, 35, 47 (bottom), 65

Bob Firth/Firth Photobank 1, 9 (top), 51, 57, 92, 96, 110–111
(bottom), 120

Henry Horenstein 6, 10 (bottom), 39 (top)

Gordon Inyard 8, 26, 58–59, 85, 114–115

Kansas State Historical Society 56

Tom Keller & Associates
John M. Mantel 30, 46, 60, 106, 111 (top), 122 (bottom)

The Kobal Collection 103, 108 (top), 110 (top), 113, 119

Light Sources Stock
James Lemass 127

Patti McConville & Les Sumner 15

Miltronics MFG., Inc/Electronic Art Division Keene, NH 72

Suzanne L. Murphy 126

Omni-Photo Communications
Jack Parsons 78

Ontario & Wells
Michael L. Abramson 83 (top)

Photo Network 123
Grace Davies 4 (bottom)

The Picture Cube
Kindra Clineff 7 (bottom), 9 (bottom)
Shaffer-Smith 94 (right)

Picture Perfect
Mark E. Gibson 71
Dave & Les Jacobs 20 (bottom)
Bill Nawrocki 64, 124–125
Brian Roberts 40 (top), 104–105

Eric Roth 38

Joan Sage 94 (left)

Don Sawyer 44, 116

Joy E. Scheller 68, 80–81

Vincent Tango 121

Unicorn Stock Photos
Jeff Greenberg 67
Jean Higgins 84

TerryWild Studio 25

Woodfin Camp and Associates, Inc.
Geoffrey Clifford 34
Jeff Lowenthal 4 (top), 83 (bottom)
Jim Wilson 104 (left)

Jonathan Yonan 10 (top), 12 (top), 20 (top), 21, 22–23, 24, 31,
40 (bottom), 47 (top), 48 (top left), 54, 75, 86, 87, 90, 93, 108
(bottom), 109, 117

Gale Zucker 17

ACKNOWLEDGMENTS

The editors and author would like to thank the following individuals
and organizations for their assistance: John Baeder, Bradford Licensing,
The Coca-Cola Company, Myles Henry at The Maine Diner, Miltronics
Manufacturing, Inc., The Pepsi-Cola Company, and Vincent Tango.

Coca-Cola, Coke, the contour bottle design, and the Dynamic Ribbon device are
registered trademarks of The Coca-Cola Company.

Pepsi-Cola and Pepsi are registered trademarks used with the permission
of © PepsiCo, Inc.

CONTENTS

INTRODUCTION

Comfortable and inviting; air that smells all at once like strong coffee, sizzling bacon, and fresh apple pie; the rousing bustle of dishes and glassware clanging along the counters; the boisterous laughter of people pressed together in booths: These are the sights and sounds of the glorious diners of America. So, too, are the neon lights, shiny silver buildings, chrome counter stools, and rollicking jukeboxes; so, too, are the blue-plate specials of meat loaf and potatoes, the lemon meringue pie, the fried chicken in the basket, and the malted milk shakes. Diners across America pay homage to the spirit and ingenuity of our earliest entrepreneurs, and celebrate the energy and passion of an American culture devoted to simple pleasures and classic, unadorned food.

WHAT DEFINES A DINER? FOOD, ARCHITECTURE, AND ATMOSPHERE

More than booths and stools, more than comfortable, friendly service, diners are beloved for offering good old fashioned "blue plate specials"—main courses ranging from fish and chips and roast turkey with cranberry sauce, to golden blintzes with sour cream.

My earliest diner memories are of Sunday visits to the Turnpike Diner in New Jersey; my mom, grandfather, three brothers, and I would squeeze into a booth, order Coca-Cola which had to last the entire meal, fight over quarters to put in the jukebox, and fill up on succulent fried chicken, served in a wicker basket and smothered in fries. In my late teens, as a camp counselor in upstate New York, the East Greenbush Diner, with its cream-cheese omelets and home-baked butter cookies (free, on a platter, near the cashier), was

White Rose System by John Baeder.
1993; oil on canvas. Linden, New Jersey.
Artist John Baeder's re-creations of diners,
such as this one in Linden, New Jersey,
illuminate the magic of these quintessential
roadside eateries.

"The diner is everybody's kitchen."

—Richard J. S. Gutman, *American Diner, Then and Now*

ABOVE
Diners fill a niche for a family-oriented eating experience that is fun, easy on the budget, and always delicious.

OPPOSITE TOP
The Cheyenne Diner, located in New York City, is a classic example of a Paramount diner, a manufacturing company known for its striking stainless-steel exteriors and Art Deco-style interiors.

OPPOSITE BOTTOM
In these days of double-tall mocha lattes, a simple cup of steaming, black coffee is sublime.

a weekly destination on days off from camp food. Later, living in New York City, diners were a source of cheap eats and late nights out with friends; we'd go to Cozy's for some pea soup and fried-egg sandwiches, or grab a cab down to the Moondance Diner for steaming coffee and mouth-watering cheeseburgers. Diners became a way to revel in the electricity and exhilaration of an all-night city.

Later still, as I moved across America, my visits to diners reflected a yearning for a simpler life: milk shakes, a plate of french fries, grilled-cheese sandwiches. It was in California that I discovered the rock 'n' roll diners, the retro diners: Johnny Rockets, The Corvette Diner, and Ed Debevic's. But whether the diners of your memories take you back to the colonial diners of New Jersey, the stainless-steel railroad-car diners throughout the Northeast, the Art Deco diners of the '50s, or the multitude of prefabricated diners along the roadsides of America, what stands true for nearly all diner lovers is the unique combination of elements that define a diner:

simple, homemade food, a distinctive and inviting design, and a sense of comfort and delight that has made diners a loyal friend to all who enter.

CLASSIC AMERICAN FOOD

Round-the-clock breakfast, low-priced specials, fast service, generous portions, and bottomless cups of coffee are the hallmarks of America's most popular cuisine. Long before the franchised fast-food places of today, diners made their mark as America's first convenience-food outlets. Before taco stands, hot-dog vendors, chili carts, burger joints, and coffee bars, the diners of yesteryear served up easy-to-prepare, tasty meals that were filling, affordable, and quick.

The original diners had little space, limited funds, and hungry, hard-working customers. If it was filling and could be prepared quickly, cheaply, and easily in a small kitchen, it was perfect diner food. All fast food of today is a descendent of the early diners; just as working folks' dungarees gave way to today's all-American blue jeans, America's earliest roadside eateries stirred a passion for cheap and filling food that has come to represent what is simple, honest, and unpretentious about America's most popular eating adventure.

DINER ARCHITECTURE

To some folks, a diner is one thing only: a stand-alone, prefabricated structure with counter service

The Salem Diner by Gordon Inyard. 1994; acrylic on board; 30 x 40 in. (76.2 x 101.6 cm). Salem, Massachusetts. Capturing the alluring images of roadside culture has become a passionate goal for many of America's artists.

and cheap eats. But some define diners more comprehensively, describing diner architecture as something that changed significantly and dramatically—in style, function, and purpose—as American lifestyles changed throughout history.

A discussion of diner architecture necessarily includes the changes in materials and forms that took place over the years. The 1920s' diner manufacturers began using stainless steel to replace wooden lunch-cart walls, and in the 1930s and 1940s, industrial designers imposed the lean qualities of emerging automobile designs on diners, developing sleeker, more streamlined diners. Formica, tile, and neon were incorporated into diner designs of the 1950s, and the fascination with space and travel to the moon in the 1960s brought further changes. Futuristic diners, complete with glass, tile, and zigzagging roofs appeared in the 1960s and 1970s, as diner builders borrowed designs from American culture to keep up with the times.

Another change in diner design resulted from America's fascination with the past. The colonial imagery took hold of some diner designers, who began replacing stainless steel with tile, adding some nautical motifs, filling other diners with brick and copper, and others with colorful crockery. Plastic-laminated, wood-grained paneling cropped up in some diners, as did cast-iron brackets and hanging plants. In keeping with diner tradition of creating a unique architectural style, some designers began experimenting with stucco, stone, mirrors, and Tiffany-style lamps, giving way to the Mediterranean-style diners of the 1970s. High-tech diners, the re-creation of old-style diners, and new versions of '30s, '40s, and '50s classics were another way to keep diners current and inviting, especially in light of the growing competition from fast-food joints and ever-growing franchises in the 1980s and '90s.

The growth and design of diners is inextricably bound to the development of America. The change in tastes and eating habits, the effects of public transportation and private automobiles, the incorporation of contemporary styles, and the entrepreneurial spirit of American workers all had their impact on the architecture and design of America's popular eateries. What remains constant about diner architecture is its emphasis on character and a down-home sensibility, as well as its place as a unique American icon and venerable art form.

This diner sign hangs as a simple and unadorned reminder of the reason diners are so popular today—everybody loves to eat! Giant roadside signs have pointed the way to good, home-cooked meals for generations of motorists along America's roadways.

Diner architecture changed significantly and dramatically—in style, function, and purpose—as American lifestyles changed throughout history. Here, the Miss Lyndonville Diner in Lyndonville, Vermont, features Tiffany-style lamps and wood-paneled interiors, a far cry from the Art Deco and stainless-steel diners that were most popular in the 1930s and '40s.

Beginning in the 1930s, the number of people traveling by automobile increased, and the idea was born to place diners along major roadways. More congenial than cafeterias and more accessible than drugstore soda fountains, the diner became the preferred eatery of choice for a nation increasingly on the move. *The Edgewood Diner, Edgewood, Maryland.*

Eating at diners is as comfortable and relaxing as a meal at home—and you don't have to clean up the dishes!

ATMOSPHERE

On a recent visit to Mel's Drive-In in California, a replica of the diner from the movie *American Graffiti*, my fellow breakfasters included an elderly, colorfully dressed couple visiting from Dayton, Ohio, two businessmen in pastel ties and shirtsleeves (nobody wears suit jackets in California), a shorts-and-T-shirt-wearing housepainter and his helper, a young woman in biker shorts, and a local family of four. Here, as everywhere, diners are a model of egalitarianism: the black-and-white-uniformed waitress greeted each of our tables with a typical, "What can I get ya, hon?" and, in a matter of moments, coffee, soft drinks, straws, and creamers of milk were plopped on all of our tables.

Some say the beauty of diners today is that they exist at all in a world of fast-food chains and four-star restaurants. Many believe diners have survived because of the entrepreneurial spirit of America, acknowledging the fact that diners are successful small businesses, often owned and operated by families. Others believe it is because, as we become more industrialized and separated from each other, there is

a greater need to find the homey comfort of a simple diner. And yet others believe it is a combination of those traits that are uniquely American that keep diners alive: the pride of ownership, the desire for a comfortable place to commune with friends and family, and the yearning for a home-cooked meal at a reasonable price.

Whatever reasons one subscribes to, nearly everyone agrees that a diner is often best described by the atmosphere and attitude created by the people who eat and work there. It is this spirit of camaraderie, this sense of familiarity, this return to home-cooked meals "like Mom used to make" that brings folks from all walks of life to diners. And it is this uniquely American diner culture that we celebrate in our chronicle of America's favorite roadside eateries.

Contrary to popular belief, big hair is not a pre-requisite to becoming a diner waitress—but it helps!

Chapter One

FROM LUNCH WAGON TO DINER

T he one-person lunch wagons of today that pull up to construction sights and factories late at night or during the wee hours of the morning are, in actuality, closer to the humble beginnings of American diners than are the stainless-steel rail-road-car diners dotting the highways. The earliest peddlers of these simple meals made their rounds in small wagons, serving homemade food to workers who labored during the evening hours—newspaper crews, club-room workers, saloon patrons, and policemen. From its modest beginnings grew a big business that reached the height of its popularity in the 1940s and '50s, and, many say, is being rekindled all across America today.

THE QUINTESSENTIAL EATING ESTABLISHMENT

Walk into any diner across America and the scene is remarkably familiar: groups of people immersed in animated conversation, chowing down on quintessential American food. Whether it's eggs, bacon, and home fries in the middle of the night, or a greasy cheeseburger for breakfast, this great American institution is known to all as a place to go where lively chatter and a big appetite are always welcome.

In the 1600s, the need to gather in a local place for food and conversation brought men to neighborhood inns to talk over world affairs. Food and drink encouraged conversation, and through conversation, they learned of new ideas,

The desire for more seating in early diner designs begat rows of counter stools running the length of the dining car. The stylish look of chrome counter stools topped with leather seats emphasized the clean, sleek appeal of diners.

Dot's Dinette by John Baeder. 1986; oil on canvas; 30 x 48 in. (76.2 x 121.9 cm). Ouray, Colorado.
This "Airstream trailer-turned-eatery" was re-created by artist John Baeder as a salute to America's " beloved shiny, silvery, movable home away from home."

"I want a dish to taste good, rather than to have been sweetened in pig's milk and served wrapped in a rhubarb leaf with grated thistle root."

—Kingsley Amis

13

new cities, and new countries. Slowly, the eating part of the inn, then called a tavern, began servicing people who were not staying at the inn, and in time the tavern became a separate business. In England, these eating establishments were called coffeehouses, and in France they were called cafés, meaning coffee. The word "restaurant" was not used until after about 1750. At first it referred only to the eating section of a hotel, or to a coffeehouse patronized by the rich. By the 1900s, the name came to be used for several types of eating places. Today it applies to almost any place that serves food and beverages.

Restaurants in the United States range from the small hamburger stand to the most expensive nightclub. They include hotel dining rooms, tearooms, sandwich shops, coffee shops, cafeterias, fountain lunches, and, with increasing frequency, beginning in the 1920s and '30s, roadside eating places called diners.

AMERICA'S FIRST ROADSIDE DINER

In 1872, a man named Walter Scott traveled around Providence, Rhode Island, in a small horse-drawn cart, offering homemade food and drinks to night workers. He was open for business late at night when all the other restaurants were closed. Known as the Providence Lunch Counter, Walter Scott's cart was a covered freight wagon with holes cut out through which he served food and collected money. By the time he retired in 1917, at the age of seventy-six, lunch carts were growing in popularity across the Northeast, and the lunch-wagon business was well on its way toward becoming a profitable and booming industry.

TYPES OF RESTAURANTS

The unique role of the diner follows a tradition of eating establishments dedicated to serving the needs of a hungry and mobile population. Other types of eateries cropped up in American cities as workers began searching for places to eat outside of the home. One type of eatery, the cafeteria, displayed its food in a large serving area as the cafeteria patron took his tray around and served himself. Automats, which originated in Germany in the late 1800s, were a kind of cafeteria operated by coins. Each item of food was displayed in a small compartment with a glass door, and one had simply to insert a coin to get the food of choice. Automats were especially popular in New York City and Philadelphia.

Another type of restaurant serving simple food was the soda fountain. First established in community drugstores, its name reflected its most popular feature. Although cafeterias, automats, and soda fountains still exist today, none of these eateries fulfilled the desires of a growing nation searching for a comfortable, inviting, sit-down place where one could get a hot, home-cooked meal.

Automats, which originated in Germany in the late 1800s, were a type of cafeteria operated by coins. Each item of food was displayed in a small compartment with a glass door, and one had simply to insert a coin to get their food of choice. Automats were especially popular in New York City and Philadelphia.

Diner Fountain Specialties

Drinks

Cherry Cola

Chocolate Soda

Pink Lemonade

Root Beer Float

Coca-Cola Float

New York Egg Cream

Shakes and Malts

Thick Ice Cream Shake

Chocolate Malt

Orange Cream

Black Cow

White Cow

Ice-Cream Sundaes

Black and White

Banana Split

Hot Fudge Sundae

Marshmallow Sundae

Strawberry Shortcake Sundae

4-Way Lunch aka Dan's Diner by John Baeder. 1993; oil on canvas; 24 x 36 in. (60.9 x 91.4 cm). Aficionados of roadside architecture revel in the character and personality that emanates from a memorable roadside diner. Here, artist John Baeder pays homage to an eleven-stool diner in Cartersville, Georgia.

INCREASING MOBILITY

Before diners became the loyal friend of the hungry, the way Americans traveled went through substantial changes. In the 1700s and early 1800s, travel was mainly on foot or on horseback. The first extensive, hard-surfaced road was 62 miles long and surfaced with hand-broken stone and gravel. By the 1830s, it appeared as though road building would boom. But then the first steam locomotive was successfully operated and rapid development of railroads began. It was not until the

Although diners originated in New England, many diner lovers argue that New Jersey is the state most known for these beloved eateries. New Jersey, home of the Trent Diner, boasts more leading diner manufacturers than any other. *The Trent Diner, Trenton, New Jersey.*

very end of the nineteenth century that the demand for good roads began, mostly for roads extending a few miles from the railroads. With the ever-growing use of the automobile after 1900, the demand arose for good roads to all places. By 1924, the United States had over 31,000 miles of concrete road, and the diner revolution was just beginning.

As Americans became increasingly mobile and prosperous, working-class families began moving from the industrialized centers of cities to less developed suburbs. Walking to work was replaced by public transportation—buses, electric trolleys, and subways. As travel time increased, and workers could no longer run home for a quick lunch or supper, they began looking for places to grab an inexpensive, quick meal. It soon became apparent to any burgeoning entrepreneur that strategically placed eateries, selling cheap, fast, home-cooked food, could become big business. In the 1930s, customers traveled increasingly by automobiles, and the idea was born to place diners along major roadways. More congenial than cafeterias and automats, and more accessible than a drugstore soda fountain, the diner became the preferred eatery of choice for a nation increasingly on the move.

Big Texan, Big Steak, Big Sign . . . this is one roadside eatery that is hard to miss! *Big Texan, Amarillo, Texas.*

NIGHT LUNCH CARS

The diner's humble beginnings took place in the late 1800s, when a man named Walter Scott hooked a horse to a small freight wagon, filled it with sandwiches, boiled eggs, pies, sliced chicken, and coffee, and ambled onto the streets of Providence, Rhode Island. An early

No one ever accused diner food of having
a slimming effect!

He may live without books, what is knowledge but grieving?

He may live without hope, what is hope but deceiving?

He may live without love, what is passion but pining?

But where is the man that can live without dining?

—Owen Meredith

This Barriere lunch wagon, built for the Haven brothers of Providence, Rhode Island, is one of Barriere's first wagons. The Haven brothers had had a White House Cafe since 1893, and decided to replace it with a brand new Barriere model.

GO WEST, YOUNG MAN

The lunch-wagon business was a growing northeastern industry in 1888,

when Thomas H. Buckley, a former lunch-wagon counter boy, built himself a lunch

wagon. He called his cart The Owl, and invited customers inside to sit at

one of the four stools in the dining area. After running his lunch-wagon business in

Worcester, Massachusetts, for several years, the first Buckley wagon was taken to Denver,

Colorado, and the budding industry began its expansion across the West.

ABOVE
The predecessor of today's diners, the horse-drawn lunch wagon, first began providing cooked-to-order food items, for a nickel, in the late 1880s. "The Owl" became a popular name for lunch wagons selling to the night-owl trade. A fully reconstructed Night Owl Lunch Car is on display at the Henry Ford Museum in Dearborn, Michigan. *Night Owl Lunch Wagon, Greenfield Village, Dearborn, Michigan.*

OPPOSITE
Diner food is the cornerstone of genuine American home-cooking, symbolizing an infatuation with simple, basic meals, fresh ingredients, and personal, hands-on preparation. Home-made pies are, to many, a slice of diner heaven.

connection with the newspaper business helped him to realize that there were newspaper workers toiling into the midnight hours. He cut holes in both sides of the wagon and proceeded to set up his moveable feast directly across from the *Providence Journal*, knowing that nighttime newspaper crews would be coming off their shifts. Before this innovation, night workers could not get anything to eat after eight o'clock in the evening, when all the restaurants closed down. His lunch wagon was a hit—not only with the newspaper crews, but also with nighttime revelers, police patrolling the street, and other hungry night workers. In no time at all there were thirty such lunch wagons in Providence alone.

The idea began to spread—one enterprising man moved from Providence to Worcester, Massachusetts, and brought the novel idea of night lunch wagons to his new community. It didn't take long for mass production of lunch wagons to take flight, and in 1891 the New England Lunch Wagon Company was created, churning out hundreds of wagons into the early 1900s. Another firm, the Worcester Lunch Car Company, began to produce lunch wagons in 1906 and continued until 1962. Legend has it that the same entrepreneur who brought the lunch wagon idea to Worcester was the first to notice a group of late-night diners gathered around a

Mike's Diner by Gordon Inyard. 1993; acrylic on board; 16 x 32 in. (40.6 x 81.2 cm). The study of roadside architecture became popular in the early 1970s, when an increasing number of diners and drive-in restaurants began to be demolished or abandoned. In an effort to preserve these landmarks, roadside enthusiasts from across the country began to photograph, draw, paint, and otherwise record diner history.

"Found a little patched-up inn in the village of Bulson. . . . Proprietor had nothing but potatoes; but what a feast he laid before me. Served them in five different courses—potato soup, potato fricassee, potato creamed, potato salad and finished with potato pie. It may be because I had not eaten for 36 hours, but that meal seems about the best I ever had."

—Douglas MacArthur, *Diary* notes

lunch wagon in the rain; he immediately realized the benefit of bringing patrons in from the foul weather. Three years later, his newfangled lunch cart emerged, complete with stools, a counter, a full kitchen, and stained-glass windows. The sit-down lunch wagon was born.

FROM MOBILE TO STATIONARY

As lunch wagons' popularity grew, community members began complaining about people hanging around the wagons during regular trading hours, blocking traffic and causing congestion. Ordinances were passed to keep the wagons off the street between dawn and dusk. Out of these restrictions, the mobile lunch carts were transformed into stationary figures—lunch-car operators rented small spaces and plopped their wagons permanently on solid ground. Not only did this exempt them from the ordinances against moving lunch carts, but it also gave them an unchanging location from which to set up and display their goods. Once settled in a loca-

THE CHURCH TEMPERANCE SOCIETY

In the late 1800s, a group called The Church Temperance Society, comprised of prominent clergy and laymen of the Protestant Episcopal Church, set out to entice working men to imbibe in a cup of coffee rather than liquor. To achieve this, they bought several lunch wagons and began offering inexpensive meals to compete with the free lunch offered in most saloons of the day. Meat, vegetables, and coffee were served for a mere dime; for a few pennies customers could get pancakes and a cup of coffee. In 1893, the Church Temperance Society moved its campaign to New York City, setting up a wagon in Herald Square. New York City's first lunch wagon was so popular that the society used the profits from its ten-cent meals to purchase a second wagon. By 1898, there were eight temperance wagons in New York City.

The Tierney diner was a standard car of its time, with a barrel roof, usually one or two rows of stools, tile interiors, and skylights. The Tierney family operated a training school where buyers of Tierney models were taught the ins and outs of diner etiquette—washing dishes, scrubbing floors, baking, ordering food, and serving meals—while their diners were being constructed.

HOMEMADE DINERS

Although most diner purists claim a diner must be prefabricated and hauled to its site, exceptions to the factory-built diner cropped up as early as the 1920s. Wilfred H. Barriere, a former Worcester Lunch Car and Carriage Manufacturing Company employee, set out to build his own diners and built several, on site, that were identical to the factory-built diners. Other on-site diners were created when reconditioned trolleys, electric streetcars, and railroad cars were converted into full-fledged diners.

Southern California became the site of a number of homemade diners, made from converted streamlined railroad cars. Edward E. Mullens converted two streetcars from the Los Angeles Yellow Line by combining the two cars with a kitchen in the center, installing stools, counters, and tables, and covering the entire complex with a roof. In San Diego, Herbert L. and Raymond E. Boggs created the Boggs Brothers Airway Diner from two railroad cars.

Other homemade diners popped up when diner owners built new, larger diners on the sites of their outgrown ones. And for entrepreneurs who lived far from the diner manufacturers, almost exclusively located on the East Coast, creating a diner on site often became a practical and money-saving solution. Many of these diners were so carefully copied from existing, factory-built diners that they are virtually indistinguishable from the originals.

tion, there was nothing to keep ambitious owners from keeping their eateries open day and night. The twenty-four-hour roadside eatery began to take its place in America's culinary history.

FACTORY-BUILT DINERS

The lunch-cart business was fast becoming a burgeoning industry. In 1891, the first patent was given for a lunch-wagon design. The patent outlined a movable unit with an enclosed body, the forward portion extending over a set of small front wheels, and the rear made narrower to stand between the tops of the high back wheels. The rear of the wagon was the kitchen, with a counter separating it from the dining room, where stools or chairs could be installed. Over one of the high rear wheels was a window for passing out food to customers; the other side had a carriage window to which one could drive up and place an order. The high wheels were a necessity born of the times: Daily trips through narrow, murky streets called for special wheels to haul the lunch wagons to their destinations.

The twenty-four hour roadside eatery began to take its place in America's culinary history in the early 1900s. Diners are known for being the one place in town where you can get a hearty breakfast any time of the day or night. The Market Diner, New York City.

"Ladies Welcome"

The diner clientele in the early 1920s was mostly men, reflecting its original purpose as a service for the working class. As a result, diners quickly developed a reputation as all-male enclaves. To encourage female patronage, and to increase profits, diners had to make subtle changes to attract ladies. Beginning with "Ladies Invited" signs in the windows, and adding touches such as flower boxes and frosted-glass windows to make women feel more comfortable, diners slowly began to search for new methods to draw in more women. Eventually, diner owners realized that one of the major drawbacks for women was the stools; women were just not comfortable perched on a stool at the counter. Manufacturers started to offer diners with booths and tables, and diners slowly became acceptable eating places for both sexes.

According to Hollywood legend, screen actress Lana Turner was discovered sipping a soda at Schwab's drugstore. Here, another starlet-to-be sits sipping an ice-cream soda at a white marble counter.

What started as a northeastern concept soon moved westward. A lunch wagon from Worcester was taken to Denver, Colorado, and the night lunch business was introduced to a new, eager-to-be-fed clientele.

In the early 1900s, diners were on their way to becoming a big business. Manufacturers started building and selling diners that were bigger—30 feet long and 10.5 feet wide—to accommodate more customers, yet still small enough for safe shipping on railways. One manufacturer, Patrick Tierney, created lavish diners with tile floors and long stretches of shining metal behind the counter. He sought out profitable locations and set up shop wherever he believed money could be made. Other manufacturers joined the bandwagon, and by the end of the 1920s, diners were popular as cheap, safe places to eat. In the 1930s, manufacturers continued to build and deliver prefabricated diners—seen as "depression-proof"—to willing entrepreneurs. One manufacturer at the time advertised diners as a "golden opportunity to become your own boss."

"We plan, we toil, we suffer—in the hopes of what? A camel-load of idols' eyes? The title deeds of Radio City? The empire of Asia? A trip to the moon? No, no, no, no. Simply to wake just in time to smell coffee and bacon and eggs."

—J.B. Priestley

The ubiquitous diner stool is increasingly the preferred seat of choice for many a diner patron. The communal counter offers a comfortable nook for the diner eating alone, the regular customer who wants to schmooze with the diner waitress behind the counter, or anyone eager to sit shoulder to shoulder with a cross-section of the American public. *Miss Newport Diner.*

RAILROAD-CAR DINERS

Converting trolley cars into diners became popular when traditional horse-drawn trolleys were replaced by electric streetcars. Lots began filling with old, discarded horse trolleys, and thrifty entrepreneurs began to convert these relics into stationary lunch wagons. But as the trolley lunch wagons became more popular, trouble followed. The qualities that had made the old, used trolleys a great opportunity for an individual with little money were the same qualities that gave lunch wagons a bad standing; the old trolleys were dark, drafty, and leaky, and not very attractive. Customers soon grew wary of entering these shady establishments. Fortunately, lunch-wagon manufacturers expanded their line of prefabricated, decorated cars during this time, and the reputation of lunch wagons as safe places to grab a quick meal was saved.

The Hi-Way Diners Club

America's love of roadside diners began in the 1920s, when the automobile lured growing numbers of people onto the open road. Originally located near retail centers, factories, railroad stations, and theaters, diners soon sprang up along highways as well. In 1928, the Hi-Way Diners Club of New England, Inc. was created with the goal of creating a chain of dining cars on the highways. They believed that with so many people traveling the new motorways, what was needed were clean, efficient places to stop and grab a bite to eat. The Hi-Way Diners Club of New England set a goal of ten diners, to be located in each of five New England states by the end of 1928. The first of their diners, complete with soda fountain, opened on May 1, 1928, in Springfield, Massachusetts.

In the 1920s, diner manufacturers strove to associate the image of a railroad dining car—clean, efficient, a suitable place to relax with companions—with their portable lunch cars. Soon, manufacturers were calling their lunch cars "dining cars" and, as with the railroad dining cars, this was soon shortened to "diner."

Later, when cities discontinued electric streetcars, retired railroad cars were similarly converted into eateries. Some capitalized on the railroad motif, creating conductor's hats and uniforms for its workers. These railroad cars as dining establishments quickly became popular, and maintained the efficiency and cleanliness that had become the hallmark of reputable diners.

ON-SITE DINERS

Although many diner buffs count only prefabricated structures as "true" diners, some homemade diners did appear as early as the 1930s and '40s that, by most accounts, were true to the diner image. With most diner manufacturers based in the East, many people across the country began constructing their own "on-site" diners, which often resembled the factory-built models. As early as 1926, some diner oper-

The proverbial cup of Joe, thick and bottomless, is a staple of American diners.

SODA FOUNTAINS

In the late 1870s, when the temperance movement led many states to prohibit the sale of liquor, the neighborhood drugstore, once the leading dispenser of alcohol, became the new promoter of carbonated beverages. In an effort to regain lost alcohol-sales revenues, drugstores created elaborate fountain areas, replacing wooden counters with granite, marble, and alabaster, and adding decorative mirrors to reflect the happy faces of satisfied customers. Walgreen Drugs, one of the Midwest's largest drugstore chains during the late '20s, featured fountain service and lunch counters. In 1929, over twenty years before he founded the McDonald's Corporation, Ray Kroc approached Walgreens with the idea of replacing their current glassware with disposable cups—and is thus credited with inventing the concept of food "to go."

ators commissioned the building of diners that were too big to move through the streets. Prior to this, diner size was governed by the methods of transportation available. First horses, then trucks, then flatcars and rail, and sometimes even ships, were used to move diners to their sites. Since the building of diners had previously been governed by transportation of parts, the building of diners on location opened up new avenues of composition and design.

Modern Diner Matchbook by John Baeder. 1977; watercolor; 16 x 19 in. (40.6 x 48.2 cm).
Matchbook cover art was popular in the 1940s and '50s as a way to advertise a diner's specialties and location. Some matchbooks had artwork and wording on both the inside and outside.

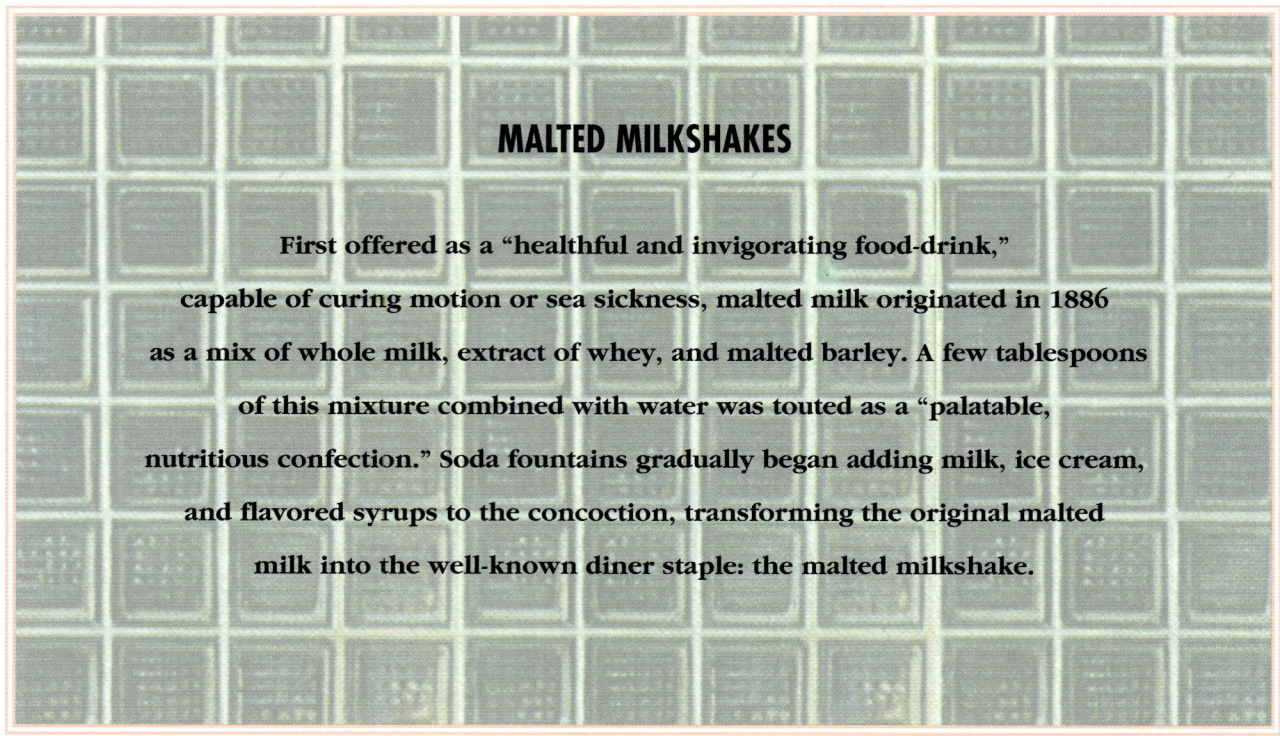

MALTED MILKSHAKES

**First offered as a "healthful and invigorating food-drink,"
capable of curing motion or sea sickness, malted milk originated in 1886
as a mix of whole milk, extract of whey, and malted barley. A few tablespoons
of this mixture combined with water was touted as a "palatable,
nutritious confection." Soda fountains gradually began adding milk, ice cream,
and flavored syrups to the concoction, transforming the original malted
milk into the well-known diner staple: the malted milkshake.**

FROM LUNCH WAGON TO DINER

The names painted across the sides of some of the earliest roadside eateries—names such as The Lunch Wagon, Quick Lunch Cafe, Rite-Bite Lunch, The Lunch Car, Eat-a-Bite Wheel Cafe, and The Lunch Cafe—described their function as providers of standard lunch fare: sandwiches, coffee, and pie. But by the mid-1920s, these "lunch wagons," as they had been known, were serving much more than lunch. Patrons could get breakfast, lunch, or dinner, and in many of the cars, they could get these meals around the clock. In keeping with the positive image manufacturers were hoping to associate with their products, the structure of a railroad dining car—clean, efficient, suitable for everyone—was projected as the image these lunch cars should have. Soon, manufacturers were calling their lunch cars "dining cars" and, as with the railroad dining cars, this was soon shortened to "diner." It is a name that stuck, and today nearly a thousand eateries across the United States have the word "diner" in their title.

The Agawam Diner in Boston, Massachusetts, is a Fodero model, known for their highly decorative, outstanding stainless-steel work. Peeking in through the windows, one can almost taste the homemade beef stew and the warm apple pie.

While some diners pride themselves on serving upscale, gourmet meals in an updated version of a classic diner, many diner enthusiasts seek out the old-fashioned simplicity of a Mom and Pop-style diner— where a clothespin system of keeping orders in line, combined with a good, dependable cook, is all that's needed to satisfy a hungry customer.

Chapter Two

ROADSIDE ARCHITECTURE

Nearly two thousand years ago, the Roman architect Vitruvius described the goals of architecture as *use*, *strength*, and *beauty*. Many aficionados of roadside architecture would add *fun* and *efficiency* to those goals in describing the classic design of a memorable roadside diner.

America's love of roadside diners began in the 1920s, when the automobile lured growing numbers of people onto the open road in search of adventure and fun. By the 1930s, more than 250 roads were developed across the United States, catering to the growing number of automobile travelers. Along with the automobile came entrepreneurs who designed roadside eateries to attract the travelers and truckers who needed sustenance at every hour of the day and night. From their role as a welcome oasis for tired travelers in the early part of this century, to the easy, unpretentious place where the long-haul trucker, the early-morning commuter, or the midnight tourist can grab a hot cup of coffee and a home-cooked meal today, diners have taken their place as a uniquely American style of roadside architecture.

TRADITIONAL DINERS

To the untrained eye, all diners are alike: stainless-steel exteriors, speckled Formica, counter service, and big neon signs. But like cars, diners come in all different styles and fashions.

Signature corners, such as this one on the Route 66 Diner, were a manufacturer's way of developing a unique look. This classic Mountain View model uses a curved glass window on top of a rounded sheet of stainless steel to set it apart. *Route 66 Diner, Springfield, Massachusetts.*

Curley's by John Baeder. 1977; watercolor.
Stamford, Connecticut.
This artistic rendering of Curley's, a Mountain
View diner in Stamford, Connecticut, captures
the stylish curves and gleaming stainless-steel
patterns of a classic diner.

"All happiness depends on a leisurely breakfast."
—John Gunther

For many diner owners, running a diner is a family enterprise. This 1920s dining car offers "perfect coffee" at Mr. & Mrs. Smith's Perfect Diners.

Starting in the early 1900s, three companies came into being which established diner manufacturing as an industry, and fathered many of the subsequent manufacturers still building diners today. The pioneers in the diner architecture trade were The Patrick J. Tierney Company, the Worcester Lunch Car and Carriage Manufacturing Company, and the Jerry O'Mahony Company. Many diners today can still be identified by their ties to their original designs, and a large number of the restored and refurbished diners today are reproductions of these original models.

TIERNEY DINERS

Tierney is credited with saving diners from the bad image associated with the unattractive, dank, converted trolleys that proliferated in the early 1920s. His cars, prefabricated on assembly lines, were equipped with tile, exhaust fans, skylights, and

DINETTES

In the early '30s, small diners became very popular. The White Castle and White Tower hamburger stands were flourishing, and diner operators began demanding small, one-man units that would allow them to stay afloat during the difficult Depression days. In response, the Kullman Dining Car company built several small "dinettes" to fill the need. The Valentine Manufacturing Company built a reputation for designing small, one-unit diners with ten stools. One model, called The Little Chef, was popular after World War II, when returning veterans were looking for inexpensive business ventures.

ventilation. Less known, but perhaps most greatly appreciated by diner patrons everywhere, is the credit he is due for a major advance in diner architecture: bringing the toilet inside.

WORCESTER DINERS

The roofline of the first Worcester diner was an innovation that set it apart from its predecessors. Until that time, almost all lunch wagons were built with barrel roofs. The earliest Worcester roof had a barrel shape when seen from the end, but had a monitor with a raised clerestory to add light to the interior, and operable windows to vent the car. The exteriors were elaborately painted, and the interiors were finished in highly varnished natural wood, with gold-leaf striping and fleurs-de-lis ceiling decoration. Wood-topped stools stood along the eating shelf. Later models were modified to include less elaborate painting, the kitchen was placed along the length of the car, and a long, inviting, eating counter ran down the middle. It was the Worcester Company that brought a further innovation to the diner industry: electricity.

Diner interiors often emulated works of art as diner designers experimented with a variety of tile patterns and designs on the floors, walls, and bases of counters.

Rosebud by Don Sawyer. Watercolor. The desire to preserve diners has inspired many artists to capture the beauty, simplicity, and sincerity of these artifacts of American history.

DINER TRANSPORTATION

Until the mid-1920s, the size of a diner was determined by the method of transport used to ship it to its desired site. The earliest diners were transported by teams of horses. Eventually, trucks replaced horses as the favored means of transportation, and diners going long distances were transported by flatcars and rail. The diner's wheels, doorknobs, and other exterior embellishments were removed, and the diner was bolted to a flatcar. At the time, the average diner was about 30 feet long and no wider than 10.5 feet, the size necessary to fit on a railroad car. For very long distances, some diners were rigged onto barges and transported by water to their new locations.

Later, diner designers opted for larger, more unwieldy designs. Diners too large to transport were built on site, or were designed in more than one section and assembled at their locations. Today, trucks and trailers are still used to move diners from one site to another. The technological advances in design, packing, and delivery have made it unnecessary for designers to be at the mercy of transportation options.

COFFEE SHOP ARCHITECTURE

Coffee-Shop Modern became a popular architectural style in the 1950s and '60s for a wide range of roadside eateries, particularly on the West Coast. Individual coffee shops and several chains, such as Denny's and Howard Johnsons, used elements of diner design such as stainless-steel fixtures, Formica surfaces, exposed grills and cooks, shiny stools and counters, and family-size booths, to create larger, more elegant eateries for the growing, car-oriented public. A more open, abstract style was applied to many coffee shops, with tall, oddly shaped signboards and plenty of glass. Although the emphasis on round-the-clock dining and simple, inexpensive meals was the same, the large, impersonal atmosphere, giant signs, and extravagantly shaped roofs helped define coffee-shop architecture as distinct from the streamlined diners more prevalent on the East Coast.

O'MAHONY DINERS

Jerry O'Mahony's architectural dream was to combine beauty and form in a diner solid enough to withstand the ruthless East Coast winters, and beautiful enough to attract the wariest of customers. His design included a barrel roof, approximately 10 feet wide by 26 feet long, with a center entrance through a sliding door. A symmetrical facade of five windows flanked the center opening. The narrow end had four windows and a side entrance. There were two operable transom windows at each end. Prior to the 1920s, the windows of an O'Mahony diner were etched with fancy, geometric floral designs. The exteriors were built with pine paneling, and the cars were custom painted with elaborate block letters and floral borders. Eventually, the O'Mahony company became the largest manufacturer of its time.

Collecting and displaying original items from early diners has become a popular hobby for many diner enthusiasts. Many diners today display these collectibles as part of their allure. *Stardust Diner, New York City.*

BARRIERE DINERS

Several new companies began manufacturing diners as the success of the Tierney, O'Mahony, and Worcester Lunch companies became

LEFT
Diners of the late 1920s became bigger and longer than their predecessors. Ted's Diner, in Milford, Massachusetts, a 1920s O'Mahony model, was a large diner for its day.

BELOW
Dazzling combinations of ceramic tile were a specialty of Tierney diners. This floor in a Tierney model is an example of artistry in mosaic tile.

WINDHAM GRILL

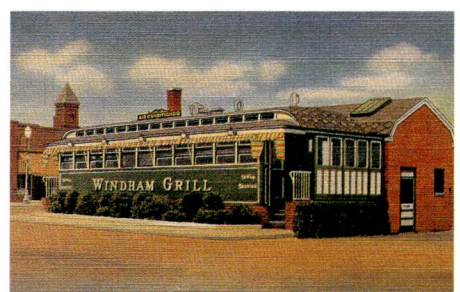

Roadside eateries stirred a passion for cheap and filling food that has come to represent what is simple, honest, and unpretentious about America's most popular eating adventure.

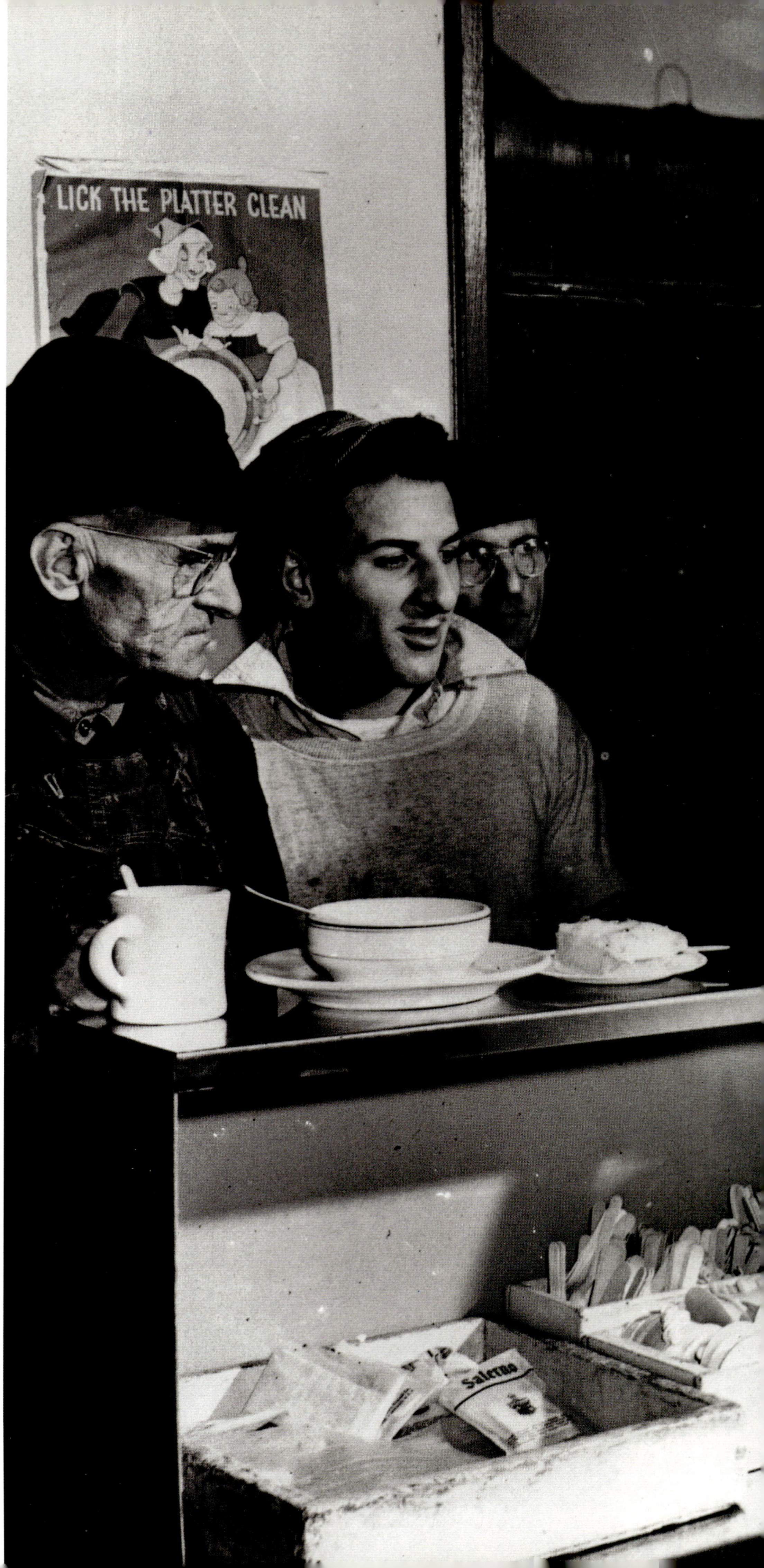
LICK THE PLATTER CLEAN
Salerno

The image of the diner as a "home away from home" for the hardworking laborer reflects its ties to the origin of diners as a male-dominated establishment.

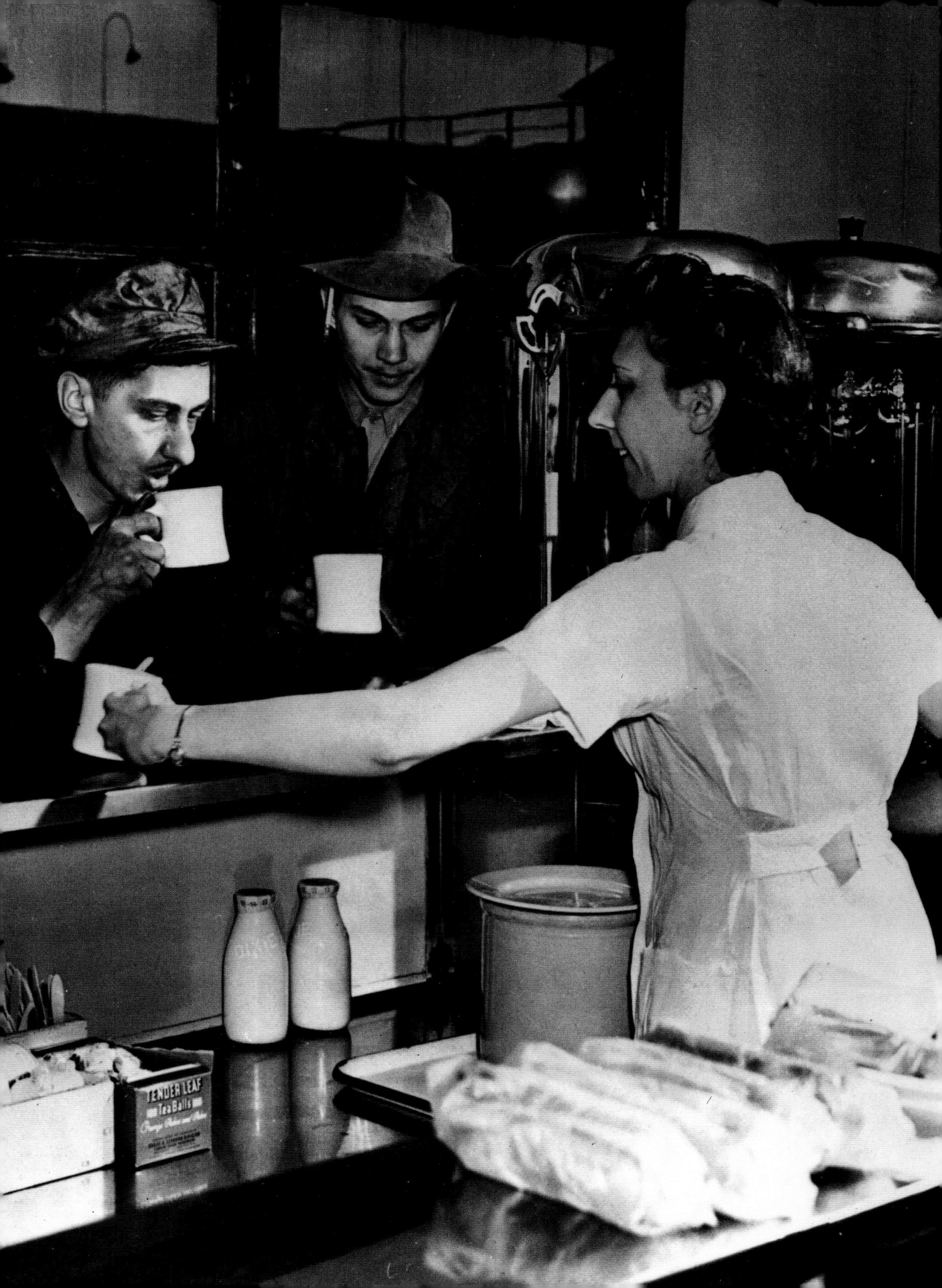

Diners were America's first convenience food outlets. Serving everything from boxed cereals to homemade pies, this great American institution is known to all as a place where big appetites are always welcome.

known. Although many folded quickly, the variety of manufacturing approaches brought a new pace to the architectural design of diners. A Worcester Lunch employee, Wilfred Barriere, started his own business, building diners in Massachusetts. Although very similar to a Worcester diner, a Barriere diner had three transom windows, as opposed to Worcester's two. On the fancy Barriere models, the windows were elaborately leaded with stained and etched glass. Although it was still difficult to tell a Worcester from a Barrier from an O'Mahony from a Tierney, the slight changes in end-window configurations and roof design began to distinguish the various architectural styles.

RECONDITIONED DINERS

"Reconditioned" diners were generally old diners that had been traded in for newer, larger ones. These used (and often poorly kept) units would be re-polished, painted, cleaned, and sold at a discount to entrepreneurs looking for a bargain in the diner industry. During the Depression years, reconditioned diners became a very popular business option.

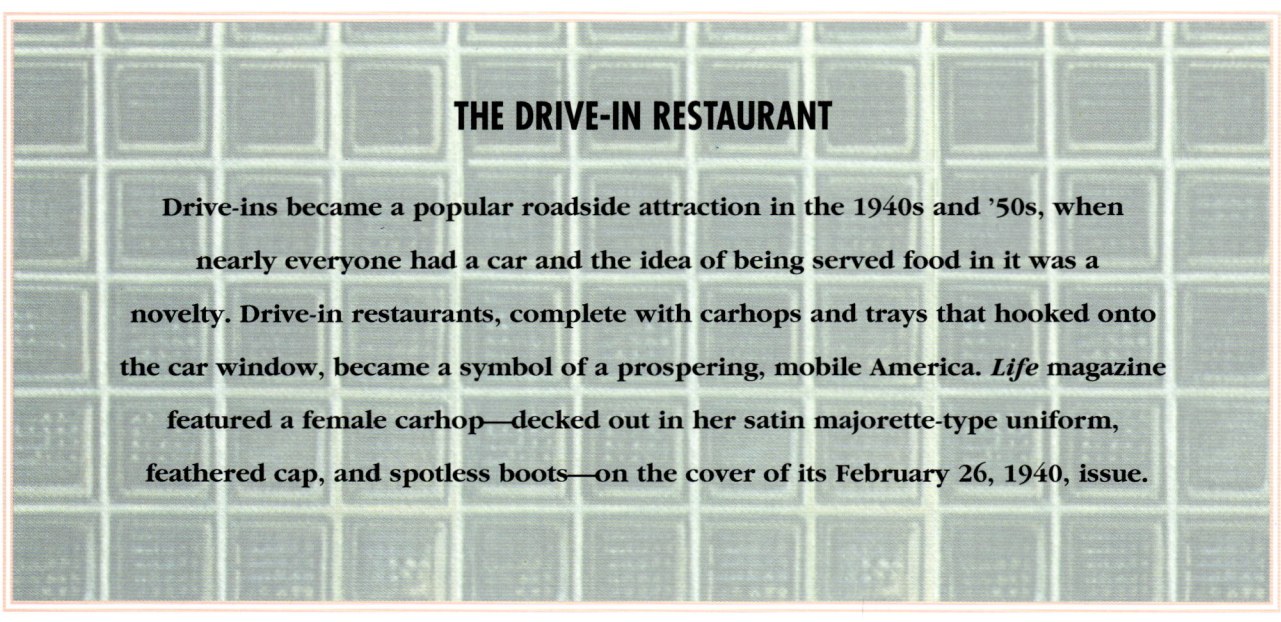

THE DRIVE-IN RESTAURANT

Drive-ins became a popular roadside attraction in the 1940s and '50s, when nearly everyone had a car and the idea of being served food in it was a novelty. Drive-in restaurants, complete with carhops and trays that hooked onto the car window, became a symbol of a prospering, mobile America. *Life* magazine featured a female carhop—decked out in her satin majorette-type uniform, feathered cap, and spotless boots—on the cover of its February 26, 1940, issue.

ABOVE
Drive-in restaurants became a symbol of a prospering, mobile America in the 1940s and '50s. Here, an innovative design eliminates the need for carhops and trays that hooked onto the car window—the food is ordered and arrives on a track alongside the car.

OPPOSITE
Homemade diners, such as the Towne Diner pictured here, were built on-site rather than prefabricated at a factory and transported to their locations. Constructed as a combination Worcester Lunch Car/Paramount Diner, with round glass-block corners and a two-toned porcelain enamel exterior, the Towne Diner is hard to distinguish from a factory-built model.

BRILL STEEL DINERS

Brill Steel Diners, built by the Wason Manufacturing Company in 1927, had a unique look. Their diners resembled railroad cars: boxy diners with monitor roofs and plain exteriors. The metal exteriors were finished in lacquer, and the interiors had ceilings and walls of porcelain enamel, tile floors, and mahogany trim. A glass eating counter, doubling as a refrigerated display of ready-to-eat fruit, salads, pies, and pastries, became a trademark of a Brill diner.

BIXLER DINERS

A distinctive roof and greater width were the calling cards for the Bixler Diners built by the Bixler Manufacturing Company in the 1930s. Bixler diners were 16 feet wide, shipped in sections on railroad cars, and erected on site. In addition to their larger size, their roofs had an unusual end trim. Bixlers were also distinguished by their double-hung, modular, 2-foot windows. Many of the newer manufacturers of large diners had difficulty keeping sales alive during the Depression years, however, and by 1937, the Bixler Company faded from the diner scene along with many others.

ABOVE
Clocks circled in neon became a regular fixture atop many diners. This brilliant display adds a touch of illuminated magic to a dark night.

OPPOSITE
Although coffeeshops developed a unique architectural style distinct from diners, the emphasis on round-the-clock dining and the bottomless cup of coffee remained the same.

"Square meals, not adventurous ones, are what you should seek."

—Bryan Miller

FORMICA: A DINER STAPLE

Formica, invented in 1913, found its way into diners in the mid-1930s.

Decorative Formica became a more durable, less expensive material for ceil-

ings, walls, and countertops, replacing metal, wood, and porcelain enamel.

With its sleek, smooth appeal, Formica soon emerged as the preferred look

for diners. By 1940, the decorative choices were numerous, with over

seventy colors and several silk-screened designs available.

This classic Valentine diner, with its profusion of stainless steel and stools perched on distinctive raised platforms, was a popular model in the 1940s and '50s.

VALENTINE DINERS

Valentine diners, advertised as "portable steel sandwich shops," were built in Kansas by the Valentine Manufacturing Company, founded in 1938. Their distinctive look included a brightly colored enamel exterior on a boxy building with flying-buttress corners, a pylon sign over the door, and bold stripes around the kitchen exterior. Valentines had steel frames covered with painted galvanized-steel panels or porcelain enamel, Formica countertops, and stools perched on a raised platform.

THE STERLING STREAMLINER

One of the designs with the most staying power mimicked sleek, streamlined locomotives. Stainless steel was tough and durable, and after the box design of the '20s, the polished, cleaner look of the '30s took over. Sterling streamlined buildings had lots of tile and Formica, stainless steel, and a clock with a circle of neon. The Sterling

ART DECO

The most elaborate diners of the early 1920s were filled with brilliant displays of glazed ceramic tile designs covering the walls and floor. The ceramic tile industry, which began producing colored glazes on tile in the late 1800s, boomed in the early 1900s, when the development of tunnel kilns furthered the automation of the tile-manufacturing business. In 1923, there were about twenty-five tile-making firms in America. As a result of the building boom after World War I, there were seventy-five ceramic-tile plants in the United States. Diner designers began experimenting with a variety of tile patterns and designs on the floors and walls, and bases of counters. Art Deco, characterized by bold outlines, streamlined forms, and variations on straight and perpendicular images, became a popular decorative style in diners during the 1920s and '30s.

Streamliner's design was a diner with one or two bullet-shaped ends. Beginning in 1936, the J. B. Judkins Company of Massachusetts, a former builder of custom automobile bodies, led the way with the new narrower, modular diners. Their distinctive, rounded-nose sections had an old-fashioned look, with transom windows, mahogany tile, and porcelain enamel ceilings and walls. Most Sterling Streamliners had a roof-mounted fin on which the name of the diner was etched. Established companies such as the Worcester Lunch Car Company introduced their own streamlined models as well. Instead of being rounded, their ends were slanted, giving the illusion of mobility, and were

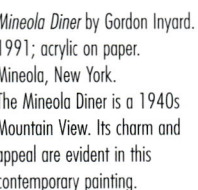

Mineola Diner by Gordon Inyard.
1991; acrylic on paper.
Mineola, New York.
The Mineola Diner is a 1940s
Mountain View. Its charm and
appeal are evident in this
contemporary painting.

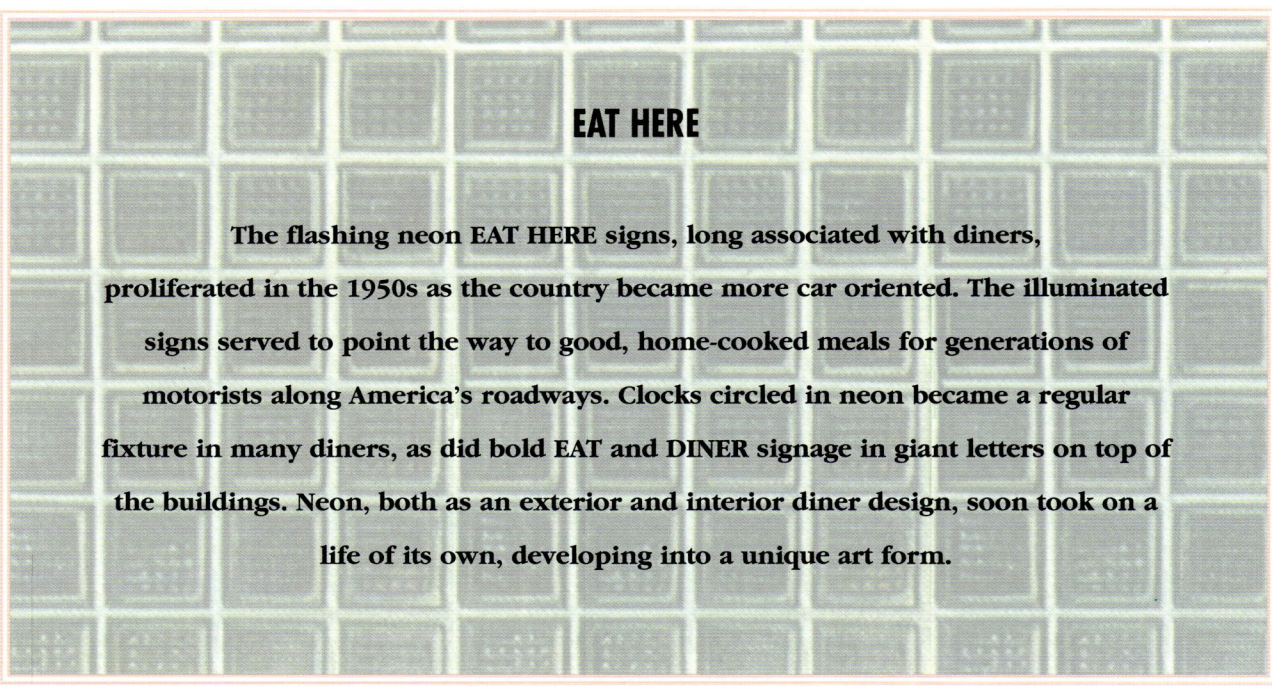

EAT HERE

The flashing neon EAT HERE signs, long associated with diners, proliferated in the 1950s as the country became more car oriented. The illuminated signs served to point the way to good, home-cooked meals for generations of motorists along America's roadways. Clocks circled in neon became a regular fixture in many diners, as did bold EAT and DINER signage in giant letters on top of the buildings. Neon, both as an exterior and interior diner design, soon took on a life of its own, developing into a unique art form.

OPPOSITE
Luminous against the night sky, this 1955 Silk City diner in Salem, New Jersey, invites customers to bask in its glow.

often given railroad names, such as the Streamliner or New Englander or Flying Red Caboose.

FROM THE 1930S TO THE '50S

The design of every building is determined by the arrangement of certain elements by an architect. It is this use of space, material, light, and style that determines how one diner is designated a Valentine, another a Tierney. In the 1930s, diners were beginning to use new materials in their designs; Formica, glass, and stainless steel began to replace wood, porcelain enamel, and metal. Stainless steel gained prominent use in diners beginning in the mid-'30s, first on the inside, replacing tile on the walls, and then on the outside, combined with porcelain enamel to create a design that is considered a classic today.

Manufacturers soon became known for their exterior styles. Paramount diners were known for glass blocks, decorative Formica, dazzling tile work, Art Deco interiors, and all-stainless-steel exteriors. These came in a variety of stainless-steel patterns: quilted, horizontal bands, and vertical creases. The emphasis was on clean, well-run establishments, with form and function going hand in hand.

Nighthawks by Edward Hopper. 1942; oil on canvas. The Art Institute of Chicago. One of Hopper's most famous works, *Nighthawks* portrays an atmospheric Greenwich Village diner in 1940s New York.

Other manufacturers gained prominence, names such as Fodero, Kullman, Mountain View, Silk City, Master, and De Raffele. Some became known for their sleekness and Art Deco design, some for their colorful metal facades, still others for their tile floors and white marble countertops. What distinguished one manufacturer from another could often be traced to a distinct window size or door design; sometimes the exterior color set it apart.

As interest in the diner trade blossomed, so did the styles and forms they took. Diner designs were copied, others were embellished with modern equipment or styles. In the 1950s, families were eating out more often, and the need for larger diners brought more changes in style. The sleek diner image gave way to a larger, family-oriented style, and once again the diner's architectural development was on the move.

DINER CORNERS

During the '50s, when diner building was at its peak, many diner designers were competing to add personal contributions to diner architecture. While some played with roof and window designs, many created a signature corner that set one diner manufacturer apart from the others.

Mountain View Diners, founded by Henry Strys and Les Daniel, built some very stylish diners with "cowcatcher" corners as a trademark. The cowcatcher corner was a curved glass window, beneath which was a cowcatcher—a sheet of stainless steel that squared off the rounded corner to a point.

Paramount Diners, founded by Arthur E. Sieber, which built a reputation for exquisite Art Deco–style diners, created a stainless-steel wedding cake for its corner, atop which sat a silver ball.

Master Diners, a small company which used stained-glass transom windows as part of its unique design, placed a double door at the corner of their diner.

Silk City Diners, founded in 1927, created a signature corner by omitting a corner window and replacing it with vertical stainless-steel sheets topped with a curved, flat panel.

CHANGING STYLES IN THE 1960S AND '70S

Beginning in the 1950s, competition was fierce for the roadside eating population. Fast-food chains, burger joints, and coffee shops began to attract many of the road-side-eatery patrons. In some regions in the 1960s, diners had to conform to rigid regulations as communities formed city planning boards to determine the look and feel of new buildings within their confines. Some places banned stainless-steel buildings; some even banned the word "diner." As a result, old stainless-steel diners began to decline in numbers. Old diners in need of repair were converted to "restaurants" by pulling down stainless-steel facades, altering windows, changing roof designs, and, sometimes, taking the word "diner" out of the name.

The Hollywood Diner in Dover, Delaware, is a 1950s-style O'Mahony diner. The stainless-steel exterior gained prominent use in diners beginning in the mid-'30s, first on the inside, replacing tile on the walls, and then on the outside, creating a design that is considered a classic today.

SPLIT DINERS

In the 1930s and '40s, the size and construction of most diners was governed by the methods of transportation used to move the fabricated diner to its site. In 1941, Paramount Diners invented the "split diner," a method of construction that enabled builders to assemble diners in two or more sections which could then be easily moved by truck or railroad. With split construction, a diner could be built in two pieces, shipped separately by rail or truck, and reassembled into one unit at its destination. Paramount was the first manufacturer to successfully design a diner that could be slit lengthwise and shipped separately, leading the way toward a future of bigger and wider diners.

INNOVATIVE DINER DESIGNS

With the rising popularity of fast-food chains, diner design took on a new and often unconventional tone. Kullman Manufacturers originated an oversized canopy running around the roofline. Some diners featured garage-style overhead doors that opened up the building in warmer months. Inspiration for new, futuristic designs came from all over; the race to the moon and the burgeoning aerospace industry were just two. Diners began appearing with ceramic tile exteriors, wide glass windows, flared overhangs, and picture-window façades.

COLONIAL DINERS

In their continuous quest to create new styles, some diner architects broke away from futuristic styles and tried to revive the classical Georgian architecture of the 1700s and early 1800s.

In the 1600s, the tavern part of an inn began offering food to people who were not guests at the establishment, and eventually the tavern became a separate business. In England these eating establishments were called coffeehouses. Here, a floating coffeehouse from the early 1700s offers food, drink, and conversation to English gentlemen.

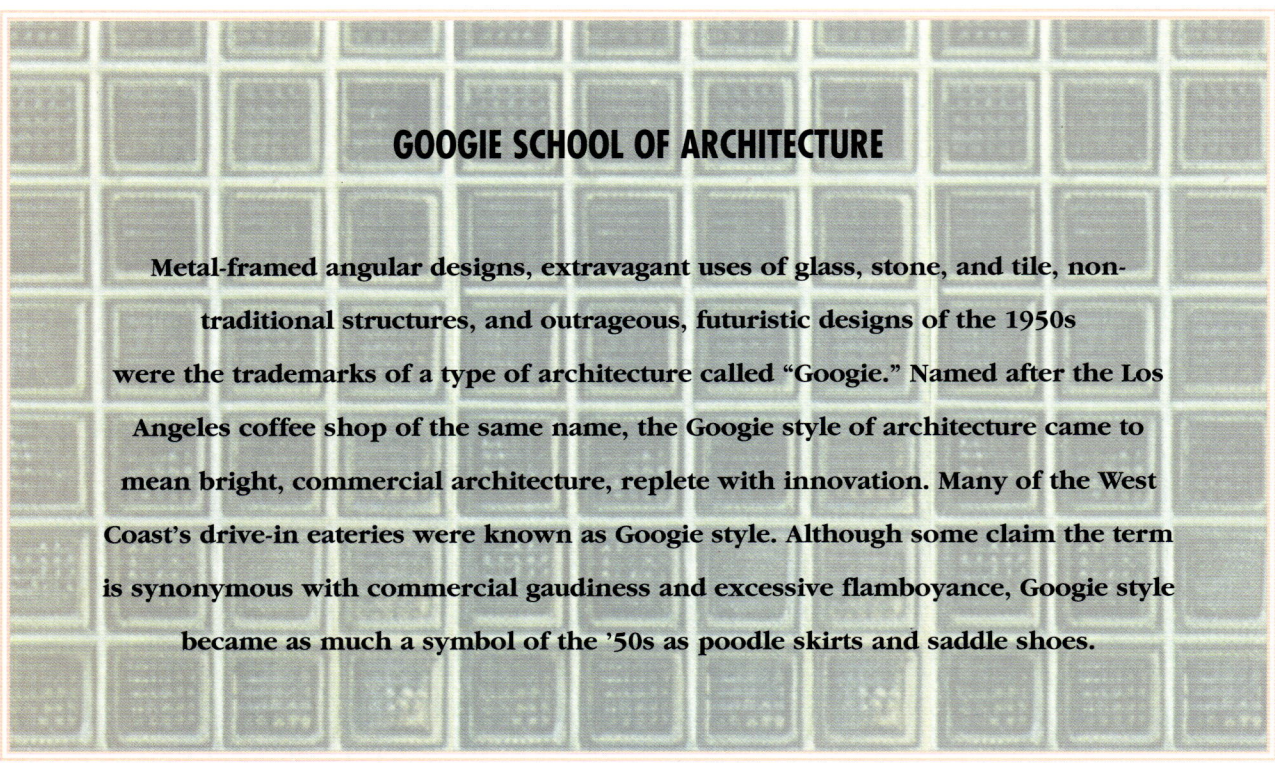

GOOGIE SCHOOL OF ARCHITECTURE

Metal-framed angular designs, extravagant uses of glass, stone, and tile, non-traditional structures, and outrageous, futuristic designs of the 1950s were the trademarks of a type of architecture called "Googie." Named after the Los Angeles coffee shop of the same name, the Googie style of architecture came to mean bright, commercial architecture, replete with innovation. Many of the West Coast's drive-in eateries were known as Googie style. Although some claim the term is synonymous with commercial gaudiness and excessive flamboyance, Googie style became as much a symbol of the '50s as poodle skirts and saddle shoes.

OPPOSITE
The craft of cooking spaghetti is elevated to an art in the hands of a master chef.

Homes in colonial times were often simple, rectangular cottages with sloped roofs to shed the snow and chimneys built of logs daubed over with clay, or brick structures with large, dignified doorways. The colonial home typically had a large fireplace and was well equipped with utensils. What emerged from this love of revival architecture were Colonial-style diners, complete with coach lamps, brick exteriors, and hanging utensils. Wood replaced much of the stainless steel, and hammered copper and wooden benches were designed to reflect early-American inns and taverns. The Colonial diner, with its emphasis on tradition and sincerity, became fashionable in the 1960s, and many of these roadside architectural structures still exist today.

MEDITERRANEAN-STYLE DINERS

The 1970s brought a revival of another classical style to diner design: Greek architecture. Using the archetypal flat roofs, stone floors, marble furniture, columns, and statues, these Mediterranean-style diners looked more like restaurants than their predecessors. The typical Mediterranean-style diner used stone and arched windows for the exteriors. Inside was a flock of new materials including carpeting,

The bright flash of neon entices passers-by to join in the warmth and comfort of a roadside diner.

smoked mirrors, scalloped countertops, Greek statues, and plum-colored Naugahyde.

MODERN DINERS

Diner builders, like the rest of the population, are influenced by the tastes and fashions of the times. In the 1980s, designers looked again to their surroundings to come up with new, high-tech diners. Using the materials of their predecessors, diner designers mixed glass, metal, stainless steel, and metal with newer materials such as granite to build larger, more elaborate, more people-friendly eateries. Established diner manufacturers such as Kullman, De Raffele, and Paramount ventured into modern-style diners, adding bronzed glass, skylights, and more polished granite and marble to older designs to create the "ultra-modern" diner designs of the 1980s.

As new and current trends proliferated in the diner industry, many yearned for the simplicity of the roadside diner of yesteryear. The newest trend to develop was the re-creation of the classic American diner, and the era of the diner revival pressed forward.

CASTLES AND TOWERS

The White Castle and White Tower restaurants were the earliest variations on the typical diner, and the first ventures into the fast-food hamburger trade. Pioneers in their own right for their unique architectural design, the White Castle and White Tower eateries began serving hamburgers and coffee along roadsides and in business districts at the same time diners were coming into their own. White Castle began in the 1920s, in Wichita, Kansas; by 1931 there were 115 White Castles selling hamburgers "by the sack." White Tower was started in Milwaukee in 1926 and had over 230 sites at its peak in the mid-'50s. Both chains were known for their all-white, one-story buildings with a castle or tower over the entrance. The medieval motifs, and the royalty in the name, reinforced the desired image of cleanliness and social prominence.

In the 1950s, the Valentine Manufacturing Company built several prefabricated buildings for the White Tower company. While the large tower, white exterior, and White Tower name gave it a distinct look, the stainless-steel kitchens, Formica countertops, ten stools, and L-shaped counter were identical to all Valentine diners. Although competition from other fast-food hamburger chains has been fierce, White Castle and White Tower restaurants, with their symbolic white designs, still remain contenders in the fast-food hamburger trade today.

A ROADSIDE CULTURAL ICON: THE GOLDEN ARCHES

To many, the arch enemies of the diner are the fast-food franchises that have cropped up in cities and on back roads and highways across America. These franchises have taken the concept of simple, inexpensive meals and focused their energies on speeding up service, cutting overhead, narrowing choices, and honing food preparation to assembly-line efficiency. By contrast, diners remained loyal to personal service, a relaxed, friendly atmosphere, and regional, home-cooked meals. The beginnings of many of these fast-food franchises, however, are closer in spirit to the early diners in their desire to give customers what they want than to the proliferation of the plastic, imitation, unoriginal fast-food stands so prevalent today. What many of these original fast-food creators responded to was the fast-car, fast-lifestyle era of a post-war America, and the desires of a growing public in search of a quick and easy place to grab a bite.

In the early 1950s, Richard (Dick) and Maurice (Mac) McDonald created a roadside eatery where customers could serve themselves at windows, each of which delivered items from the simplified menu of hamburgers, french fries, ice cream, and drinks. They offered low prices, fast service, and the opportunity to eat in one's favorite place: the car. Their success led them to design a look that would do what diners and their neon signs had been doing along the roadsides of America: grabbing the attention of a driving population in search of an easy, inexpensive roadside meal. Richard McDonald thought up an eye-catching architectural design: two giant arches.

The original McDonald's, with its dramatic shape, flaring roof, and high, golden arches, was built in May 1953 in Phoenix, Arizona. In August of 1953, a second McDonald's was built in Downey, California. In 1954, a milkshake-machine salesman from Chicago named Ray Kroc proposed the idea to the McDonald brothers of franchising the stands throughout the United States. Kroc made a deal, and opened his first McDonald's franchise in Des Plaines, Illinois, in 1955. The present McDonald's Corporation, founded by Kroc, dates one year one from this stand.

While many credit the success (and, to many diner lovers, the desecration) of the popular roadside eatery to Kroc, the oldest remaining McDonald's, in Downey, Los Angeles, built prior to Kroc's reign, was granted eligibility in the prestigious National Register of Historic Places, signifying its importance in American roadside architectural history.

While some see the growth of franchised fast-food outlets as the beginning of the end for Mom and Pop-style diners, the significance of the McDonald brothers' success has gained the franchise a notable place in American roadside architectural history.

"I have known what it was like to be hungry, but I always went right to a restaurant."

—Ring Lardner, Jr.

Chapter Three

A DINER RENAISSANCE

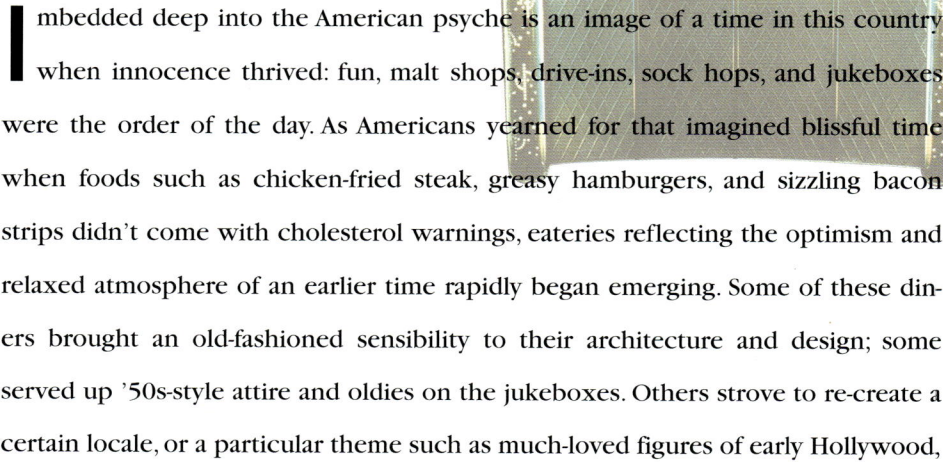

Imbedded deep into the American psyche is an image of a time in this country when innocence thrived: fun, malt shops, drive-ins, sock hops, and jukeboxes were the order of the day. As Americans yearned for that imagined blissful time when foods such as chicken-fried steak, greasy hamburgers, and sizzling bacon strips didn't come with cholesterol warnings, eateries reflecting the optimism and relaxed atmosphere of an earlier time rapidly began emerging. Some of these diners brought an old-fashioned sensibility to their architecture and design; some served up '50s-style attire and oldies on the jukeboxes. Others strove to re-create a certain locale, or a particular theme such as much-loved figures of early Hollywood, or vintage Western memorabilia. The desire to resurrect an earlier time, coupled with efforts to preserve those eateries that had managed to remain alive, created a renewed interest in diner culture all across America. A diner renaissance, involving the restoration of old diners and the creation of new "old" diners, began in earnest.

The diner is as much an icon of American way of life as the ol' red, white & blue.

DINER NOSTALGIA

The study of roadside architecture became popular in the early 1970s, when an increasing number of diners and drive-in restaurants began to be demolished or abandoned. No longer able to compete with the grow-

Shorty's Shortstop by John Baeder.
1985; oil on canvas.
In this fantasy diner, artist John Baeder
imbues a dilapidated old bus with diner-esque
qualities, making many wistful for what
might have been.

"Life itself is the proper binge."

—Julia Child

ABOVE
America's move to suburbia in the late 1940s and early '50s fueled a passion for roadside dining as never before. Mel's Drive-In, renowned as the local hangout in the movie *American Graffiti*, serves as a meeting spot for young and old alike.

OPPOSITE
Chroniclers of roadside architecture glorify the structures created to serve the motorist. Here, a diner sign dominates the roadside horizon.

ing numbers of fast-food franchises, many of these roadside eateries were left to decay, or were torn down to make way for larger, more lucrative establishments.

In an effort to preserve these landmarks of earlier centuries, roadside enthusiasts from across the country began to photograph and record the history of these buildings before they were lost. Some people professed an interest in preserving the architecture; others felt nostalgic for these establishments which symbolized simpler times. Some described a certain integrity in preserving and restoring roadside diners. Many were intrigued by the answers they believed diners provided about America's earliest entrepreneurs. *Roadside*, a quarterly magazine first established in 1990, claims it is motivated by the desire to "get Americans out of the franchises, the

Known as America's Main Street in its infancy, Route 66, along with its roadside eateries, was the road that tied much of the nation together in the 1920s and '30s. Although some of Route 66 exists today as only fragments, several state and national organizations are making efforts to insure Route 66's survival. *The Route 66 Cafe, Santa Rosa, New Mexico.*

malls, the interstates, bland suburbia, and back into the real things that foster community: diners, drive-ins, trains, porches, and anything locally owned."

What unites these diner devotees is their belief in the importance of the roadside diner in America's social history. There is little doubt that the affection for these buildings stems, in part, from the ability of these sites to arouse the collective memory of a time gone by.

ROUTE 66

U.S. Route 66 is a road that has been celebrated in song and revered in literature. Begun in the mid-1920s, it was known as America's Main Street, a road that tied much of the nation together. Although some of Route 66 exists today as fragments or as a service road, there are state and national organizations dedicated to seeing that Route 66 survives. Of its ties to the great American roadside diners, Michael Wallis, author of *Route 66: the Mother Road*, says, "Route 66 . . . is for those who are willing to sample chili from a stranger's pot, slurp root beer floats out of frosty mugs, or tackle a burger platter that requires at least a dozen napkins to sop grease off hand and chin."

Route 66, commissioned in 1926, was the first highway to link Chicago with Los Angeles. By the mid-1930s, the highway had already begun to symbolize a journey; the notion of being out on the open road was grabbing the hearts of an increasingly mobile America. Author John Steinbeck termed Route 66 "the mother road." Singer Nat King Cole recorded the song "Route 66" and made it a household term for a place to "get your kicks." During the 1960s, the successful TV series *Route 66*, created by Stirling Silliphant and Herbert B. Leonard, gave the highway additional fame and prominence. In the process, Route 66 became more than a way to travel from state to state—it became an emblem of freedom, a route to better times and renewed hopes. As new, fast-moving freeways began to dot the country, however, Route 66 was fast on its way toward becoming another outdated, abandoned roadway.

The last several years have seen a surge of interest in Route 66. State and local associations, and the National Route 66 Association, formed in 1983, have made substantial efforts to revitalize the highway. The spirit of America, long associated with traveling by automobile, is being rekindled through this revitalization, along with the resurgent interest in the inviting eateries that dot its roadsides.

DINER ART

Artist John Baeder, author of *Diners,* travels the country photographing and documenting diners. His paintings, watercolors, and writings about diners illuminate the magic of these quintessential roadside eateries. He has been described as "a painter-poet who makes us see the beauty of common things." His blend of history, fact, re-creation, and imagination in his documentation of diners have made him a folk hero among diner lovers everywhere.

RE-CREATED DINERS

New versions of '30s, '40s, and '50s classics have sprung up all across America. Some established diner manufacturers such as Kullman were commissioned to re-create diners of the past. In 1981, a 1930s O'Mahony-style diner was built with its requisite '30s windows, stainless-steel roof, and graphic designs. A '50s diner in Washington, D.C., built by the Kullman Manufacturing Company in 1988, was a re-creation of one of their own original '50s diners. The interiors of many of these diners are designed as a remembrance of the past, with fun memorabilia from the times adorning the walls, such as references to historical events, '50s pop music, and waitresses wearing poodle skirts. Some diners re-create red-and-white vinyl booths, black-and-white tile floors, traditional soda fountains, and nostalgic beverages such as cherry or vanilla cokes. What these diners seem to be offering is more than just old-fashioned food; many seem to be attempting to recreate old-fashioned values and old-fashioned socializing.

Some themed diners celebrate the union between cars and roadside eateries, such as this one in New Mexico, in which a vintage Bel Air and other diner memorabilia adorn the wall. OL'D Diner, Espanola, New Mexico.

Empire Diner by John Baeder.
1976; oil on canvas. New York City.
John Baeder's painting captures the mood
and detail of this classic New York eating
establishment.

"The character of a diner builds up
the way grime does."

—Douglas Yorke

The local diner often serves as the favorite gathering spot for friends to swap stories, catch up on gossip, or share the big issues of the day.

RE-CLAIMED DINERS

Although many diners were demolished to make way for the new, the resurgent interest in all things old allowed many diners to be saved from destruction. Since, by design, many of the old-time diners were transportable, some of these old relics were bought and moved to new sites. Many were restored to their original appearance, slightly modified to suit the 1990s patron.

The early success of some of these restored diners blazed the way for others to find abandoned diners and restore them to their original look. One diner devotee bought a Silk City diner slated for demolition, acquired original parts from other Silk City diner owners, reassembled the diner, and successfully restored it to its original luster. Re-claiming old diners became a hobby for many diner enthusiasts, and for some, a lifelong crusade.

An enthusiastic patron embraces one of a diner's many delights.

DINER SCULPTURE

The sculptor George Segal is well known for his life-size, cast figures. During the early 1960s he began creating his direct-cast plaster figures, which were usually white with an occasional prop or piece of clothing. One of his most famous sculptures is a large work titled *The Diner*, in which the white plaster figures are set in rooms with actual stools, counters, and diner fixtures.

THEMED DINERS

Themed diners, commemorating everything from automobiles to drive-ins to bubble-gum-smacking waitresses, have cropped up in recent years. Some celebrate the union between cars and roadside eateries, adopting such names such as The Corvette Diner or The T-Bird Diner. These establishments often showcase lovingly restored classic cars; several diners sponsor classic-car nights, where proud owners bring their restored cars for all to see and admire. Many of these themed diners are chains, establishing themselves in several cities across America. One '50s-themed diner, Ed Debevic's, with several sites across America (including Los Angeles, Arizona, and Chicago), is designed around the adventures of its imaginary owner, who is widely quoted but never seen. Waitresses and busboys perform as '50s caricatures, complete with gum chewing and table hopping, as they mingle with customers.

A visit to Ed Debevic's entails more than just good food. Cluttered with 1950s memorabilia, as well as quotations from the mythical Ed, this entertaining franchise offers gum-smacking waitresses along with old-fashioned burgers and milkshakes.

WEST COAST DRIVE-INS

Many say that what the diner was to New Jersey, the drive-in was to California. With the car-oriented lifestyle of the West Coast, the architecture of California's roadside eateries was not only a cultural expression of the time period, but also a deliberate attempt to meet the functional problems of a car-oriented society, as well as the warm weather of the West Coast. Early drive-ins in Los Angeles and Texas responded by shaping roadside eateries around the need to accommodate many cars. The warm climate allowed West Coast drive-ins to be built of lighter materials such as wood and stucco, instead of the brick or stone preferred in harsher climates. Neon, a staple of East Coast diners, became an integral architectural element in the West Coast eateries as well. With its emphasis on open space, light, and circular design—which permitted access from all directions and allowed cars to converge like the spokes of a wheel—the roadside drive-in of the '30s was the West Coast's answer to the East Coast diner.

RIGHT
The Zesto Drive-In in Atlanta, Georgia, utilizes several eye-catching elements such as the clock circled in neon, a shimmering stainless-steel exterior, and a colorfully-designed neon sign to attract its clientele.

OPPOSITE
Diner Sign by Gordon Inyard, 1990; watercolor on paper. Queens, New York. Although many restaurants took the word "diner" out of their names when interest in this type of eating establishment waned during the 1960s, this diner proudly displays its nomenclature.

A glass eating counter, doubling as a refrigerated display of ready-to-eat fruit, cereals, and
pies, became the trademark of a Brill diner.

"When poets . . . write about food it is usually
celebratory. Food as the thing . . . itself, but also
the thoughtful preparation of meals, the serving
of meals, meals communally shared in a sense of
the sacred and the profane"

—Joyce Carol Oates

This example of diner etiquette—a hat-topped stool—suggests to new patrons that they'd really be better off at another seat!

Whether it's a '50s Corvette, a '60s drive-in, '20s-railroad-style uniforms, or gum-smacking waitresses, the images re-created by these themed diners have rekindled a spirit in all things nostalgic in a large segment of America's eating industry. As a restaurant industry maneuver, establishing themed diners has been a successful enterprise.

LANDMARK DINERS

Nationwide, classic diners are being hailed as artifacts worthy of preservation. The National Register of Historic Places, a federal listing of architecturally and historically

'50s KITSCH

Kitsch, generally considered to be something that appeals to popular
or low-brow taste, was at its peak in the 1950s. Artificial silks, plastic pink
flamingos, plastic flowers, and man-made fabrics were all the rage during the
'50s, and their impact on diner design was considerable. The appeal spread to
both the exterior design of diners—crazy shapes, stucco walls, and lavish
uses of glass, stone, and tile—and to the interior, with decorations such as
leatherette booths, novelty signs, and artificial plants. The optimism and
flamboyant pop culture of the '50s and '60s gave rise to a kitsch aesthetic, and it
is this flashy and optimistic innocence which is being refashioned in many of
the retro-diners flourishing across America today.

significant properties, has recognized the importance of diners as part of America's history. State and local districts have granted landmark status to several diners, and several museums have added diners to their collections of twentieth-century artifacts.

Lamy's Diner, an original 1946 Worcester semi-streamliner, was restored to its factory-built condition and is now on display in Dearborn, Michigan, in the Henry Ford Museum's exhibition "The Automobile in American Life." Visitors can enter the diner and sit at the counter or a booth. An original Worcester Lunch Car was donated to the Worcester Heritage Preservation Society and put into use as an information booth on the Worcester Common. The Orange Empire Railway Museum in California has the Liberty Bell Cafe, a Pullman passenger car that was converted to a streamlined diner in the 1930s. A reconstruction of the inside of a Valentine Diner, fabricated by a former employee of the company, is in the Kansas Museum of History. And the Savannah College of Art and Design

OPPOSITE
A miniature stainless-steel Empire State Building adorns the roof of the Empire Diner, a well-known East Coast landmark. *The Empire Diner, New York City.*

This "Franciscan Starburst" dishware was once a popular diner item.

in Savannah, Georgia, has a restored 1938 Streamliner and a 1950s Mountain View in working condition. A converted trolley is now a fixture in the Adirondack Museum in New York. Bob's Big Boy in Culver City, which opened in 1949, underwent extensive renovation in the last two years and has been restored to its former 1950s splendor. It is now a historical landmark in Burbank, and is a California "Point of Historical Interest."

From east to west, diners are being noted for their architectural, historical, and cultural significance, and are being granted places of honor in America's history.

UPSCALE DINERS

While many re-created and restored diners also re-create the simple foods and prices of an earlier era, other establishments are keeping the image of the diner, with its architectural flourishes such as the stainless-steel exterior and railroad-car shape, and modifying it for a growing upscale clientele.

THE DINER FRANCHISE BOOM

Their advertisement reads, "Build Your Future On The Past." Although large-scale franchises have been the curse of many a diner lover's dream, the growing trend in diner rebirth is in the duplication of the idealized version of a typical '50s-style diner. One company, The 5 & Diners Franchise Corporation, which operates diners in California and Arizona and has plans to open franchises in Colorado, Tennessee, and Nevada, advertises their diner as "a place to leave the cares of the world behind and groove to your favorite music. Breakfast, lunch or dinner . . . even original '50s tunes played on a vintage jukebox." As the diner becomes rediscovered, retro-diners invite the American public to relive memories or to experience a legendary time period. While some people deplore these franchised diners as commercial and crass, many say the publicity and attention generated by these new restaurants has helped traditional diners stay in existence. Fewer old diners are being demolished, and original diners are increasingly taking their place in museums and as historical landmarks.

A well-known East Coast example of this type of diner revival is the Empire Diner in Manhattan. Originally a 1946 Fodero diner, the Empire has been modified with a gigantic "EAT" sign on the wall, a miniature stainless-steel Empire State Building on its roof, and a pricier and less traditional menu. A 1954 Mountain View Diner, moved in 1984 to Cincinnati, Ohio, was re-opened as a glitzy, non-traditional diner in 1984. The Fog City Diner in San Francisco, opened in 1985, used classic diner materials and was inspired by traditional diner layouts, compete with black-and-white checkerboard tile and lots of stainless steel. Yet it veers markedly from tradition in serving upscale, gourmet meals rarely associated with old-style diners.

While many decry the direction of these new, upscale eateries, claiming that they are more "restaurant" than "diner," others see these "neo-diners" as evidence

Tabletop jukeboxes help create an old-fashioned sensibility in many roadside eateries. Vintage jukeboxes, along with Coca-Cola memorabilia, are popular diner collectibles.

"It is beyond the imagination of the menu-maker that there are people in the world who breakfast on a single egg"

—Melvin Maddocks

that diners, like all great styles of architecture, are constantly evolving. The enormous popularity of these establishments, and their continued expansion across the country, is proof that these new styles have their place in America's culinary heritage.

DINER MEMORABILIA

The enticing allure of colorful neon jukeboxes and wall decorations such as these has done much to further the popularity of diners.

A love of all things nostalgic has become an almost inevitable companion to the many restored and re-created American diners, including classic movie posters, road signs, jukeboxes, Coca-Cola bottles, neon clocks, soda fountains, '50s attire, classic cars, and penny candy. While some items decorating diners today are imitations of original products, many diner devotees pride themselves on collecting and displaying original items from the 1930s, '40s, and '50s. The most popular diner collectibles, vintage jukeboxes and Coca-Cola signs, have become standard items in most of the retro-diners of the 1990s.

JUKEBOXES

The jukebox, prior to the 1930s, was known as an "automatic phonograph." As neighborhoods began establishing diners as neighborhood gathering spots, the automatic phonograph, operated with a coin in a slot, became a focal point at these diners, for music lovers of all ages. Following the introduction of electrical amplification in 1927, the jukebox provided Americans with an introduction to a wide variety of musicians as they stopped in for a hamburger and a shake. By the 1940s, the Wurlitzer Company became the leading manufacturer of juke-

JUKEBOX MANIA

The jukebox originated in 1877, when Thomas Edison invented a sound-recording machine and sold the rights to manufacture his discovery. In 1889, the first coin-operated phonograph was installed in The Palais Royale Saloon in San Francisco, California. This early jukebox had four listening tubes; each listener could put a tube to his ear, and each required a nickel for two minutes' worth of music. By 1890, the first commercial records were made, and by the late 1890s, patrons could hear up to fifteen hundred selections through an ear tube at a phonograph parlor.

What many consider the true forerunner of the modern jukebox was The Gabel Automatic Entertainer, a coin-operated music machine invented in 1906. The Entertainer offered several selections, had its record-changing mechanism viewable through three glass sides, and a 40-inch horn that amplified its sound so that the listening tubes were no longer needed. This machine and its imitations dominated the coin-operated phonographic industry through the late 1920s.

In 1927, the first electrically amplified multi-selection phonograph was released. This technical improvement meant the jukebox could compete with orchestras and could entertain large groups in big spaces, all for the price of a nickel. Within a decade, there were at least a half-million jukeboxes across America, reaching a peak in the late 1940s and '50s, when The Wurlitzer Company introduced the hundred-song jukebox. Jukeboxes surged in popularity after World War II, when vinyl records and hi-fi sound became widely available. Table-top jukeboxes became standard issue at most of America's diners. With the decline of the diners, however, and the rise of fast-food chains, many of the classic diner jukeboxes, with their wooden cabinets, illuminated plastic designs, and bright, modern deco lines, have faded from sight. A new generation of high-tech jukeboxes, in digital form on a hard disk drive, is being launched as the "twenty-first-century jukebox."

DINER ADVERTISEMENTS

Diner advertisements from the early 1900s to the present day boast plenty of reasons to visit a particular diner. From their "reasonable prices" to their "best coffee in town," most diners had a catchy phrase to entice diners to come in for a bite. Here are some examples:

"Good Food is NOT CHEAP. Cheap Food is NOT GOOD.
We serve Good Food at Reasonable Prices."
—People's Diner, Montrose, Pennsylvania, 1960

"For All Ye Hungry Folk.
You are now eating in the Finest Dining Car in The Country."
—Flying Yankee Dining Car, Lynn, Massachusetts, 1927

"The Goods Are Right and Cooked in Sight"
—Queensborough Lunch, Gloversville, New York 1916

"The Place to Meet is The Place To Eat"
—The Squire Diner, West Chester, Pennsylvania 1953

"The World's Longest Diner"
—Elkton Diner, Elkton, Maryland, 1954

"Eat Heavy."
—Tick Tock Diner, Route 3, Clifton, New Jersey, 1947–Present

boxes; their promotional campaign in the mid-'40s delivered jukeboxes to diners all across America.

COCA-COLA ARTIFACTS

Coca-Cola, invented in 1886 by Dr. John Styth Pemberton, was originally intended to cure headaches and provide energy. When Pemberton sold his rights to businessman Asa Candler in 1892, the Coca-Cola Company blossomed into a thriving enterprise.

The Coca-Cola Company quickly mounted an aggressive marketing campaign, complete with colorful fountain signs, decorative advertising clocks, posters, calendars, and serving trays. Bell-shaped glasses imprinted with the Coca-Cola logo were added to the free samples provided to roadside eateries, and soon Coca-Cola was a highly recognized brand at virtually every diner and soda fountain in the country. By the time the distinctive bottle became a registered trademark in 1960, Coca-Cola was widely associated with classic diner food.

"It's much more than just a place to grab a bite."

—Richard J. S. Gutman, *American Diner, Then and Now*

Chapter Four

AN AMERICAN INSTITUTION

HISTORIC ROUTE 66

The original diners were a vision of utopia along America's roadsides: the aroma of home-cooked meals, the flash of shiny metal, the promise of a bottomless cup of steaming, fresh coffee. The imagery of the diner, complete with french fries, Formica counters, jukeboxes, and wise-cracking waitresses, has become a part of America's identity, a link to a time in history when Americans reveled in a sense of youthful exuberance, travel, and adventure. Revered by diner devotees, honored by those who search the country for old diners to buy and restore, the original diners of America's past have been singled out for their historic importance, their architectural relevance, and their cultural significance. The concept of diners, the enlightenment gleaned from America's affection for the simple, roadside eatery, has been extolled in numerous works of art and literature, and has earned its place as an icon in the chronicles of American culture.

The morning routine at this New Jersey diner includes a cup of coffee, the daily paper, and a subdued yet friendly smile.

MYTH OR REALITY

The concept of diners, for much of America, is as much myth as reality; a diner is often more a symbol of a way of life, like

Whitey's Diner Hotpoints by John Baeder.
1977; watercolor.
In John Baeder's painting of a trolley diner
from the late 1920s, the sparkling clean
spatulas, face down on fresh, folded towels,
await their chance to perform atop these
immaculate 1954 Hotpoint grills.

"They reminded me of temples that had sort of shot up from the ground."

—John Baeder, artist, photographer, and writer

BLUE PLATE SPECIALS

According to the *Whole Pop Catalog,* during the Depression, a manufacturer started making a plate with separate sections for each part of the meal, similar to the modern-day TV-dinner tray. Because it was inexpensive and saved on dishwashing, diners began using these dishes for their low-priced daily specials. Although the plates were eventually manufactured in various colors, the original plates were blue, and the name stuck.

In restaurants across America, a "blue plate special" has come to mean a main course with all the "fixin's"—meat, potatoes, and side dish—offered at a special price. While regional specials vary, the most popular blue plate specials seem to crop up at diners everywhere.

Blue Plate Specials—served with choice of soup or salad, potatoes, fresh vegetables, bread, and butter, and a bottomless cup of coffee:

Meatloaf and Potatoes

Chicken-Fried Steak

Beef Stroganoff

Hungarian Goulash

Pot Roast

Beef Stew

Stuffed Green Peppers

Corned Beef and Cabbage

Beef Brisket

Lasagna

Liver and Onions

Spaghetti with Meatballs

Swedish Meatballs

Veal Cutlets

Pork Chops

Chicken Cacciatore

Chicken Pot Pie

Fried Chicken

Roast Turkey

Macaroni and Cheese

motorcycles and cowboys and fast cars, than a place to grab a bite to eat. What

becomes part of the fabric of American life is often what is seen in the movies, on

television, in literature, or in advertising, and diners have become a vital part of that

fabric.

  The diner as an image has taken on several different roles in America's history.

Some define the diner by its time period, using the image of the diner to represent

a simpler, less complicated time in America. Others see the diner as an image of the

working class, symbolizing the hard-working, no-nonsense nature of the laborer or

Diners in films often serve as a revealing back-drop to a host of people and events. In *Pulp Fiction*, the film begins—and ends—with a pivotal diner scene, a critical moment in the lives of the main characters.

103

truck driver. Still others use the diner as a symbol of youth—the diner as a place to cruise up to in a glitzy car, to meet and spend hours into the night talking with a group of friends. And yet others see diners as a symbol of what has remained unchanged in an era of rapid metamorphosis in America, a place where you can still get a simple, unpretentious meal, in a simple, unassuming locale.

When asked to define a diner, people are just as likely to conjure up the drive-in from the film *American Graffiti*, or the truck stop known as Rosie's Diner (from the television commercial extolling "the quicker picker-upper"), or the diner from the television show *Roseanne*, as they are to describe a diner that they have actually visited in the recent past. A celebration of the diner as a cultural institution is a tribute to the ideas and images embedded in the American experience, as well as a recognition of what is uniquely American.

A PATHWAY TO THE PAST

The diner experience, for many, is inextricably tied up with images of sock hops, drive-ins, hot rods, James Dean, and Elvis—the diner as a reminder of a more innocent time in America is a common focus of diner lore. The rebirth of the '50s-style diner, complete with vintage oldies on the jukebox, servers dressed up in 1950s attire, and mealtime favorites such as hamburgers, french fries, and milkshakes, is still going strong, filling a need for a family restaurant that is fun, budget conscious, and entertaining. These retro-diners have proven successful all across America, suggesting that the diner as a symbol of a time gone by is widely accepted as the most popular image of American diners. The nostalgic ambiance, evidenced by '50s automobiles, fashions, and oldies music—on television, in films, and in growing numbers of malls and shopping-center eateries—is evidence of the diner's large impact on the American dining experience.

OPPOSITE
The food served up at diners across America, from meatloaf and gravy to a sandwich with coleslaw, reveals a society captivated by the simplicity and goodness of an unpretentious meal.

"Customers Like Women Better"

Although the diner waitress has become an American institution, early diners were almost entirely owned and operated by men. It wasn't until after World War II, when women were needed to replace lost manpower, that diners began using women as waitresses. In a 1941 issue of a magazine called *The Diner,* an article by diner owner Sam Yellin gave the following reasons for having an all-female staff operate his diner.

1. Women will work for less pay
2. Women don't stay out late drinking and then call in sick the next day
3. Women belong around food
4. Women will work harder than men
5. Women are always happy
6. Women are more honest than men
7. Women clean diners better than men
8. Women are cleaner than men
9. The customers like women better
10. Customers don't swear in front of women

BLUE-COLLAR DINING

Another celebrated diner image reflects its ties to the origin of diners as a working-class, male-dominated establishment. The first lunch wagons and diners of America's history were often operated by tradesmen who wanted to work for themselves. Shoemakers, carpenters, stonecutters, butchers, and janitors filled the ranks of lunch-cart operators, providing an environment that was comfortable for their often low-paid, working-class patrons. As American workers became more mobile and diners took to the highways and back roads, these roadside eateries became the haven for truck drivers who traveled

At the end of a long day on her feet, a New York City waitress counts her tips. *Market Diner, New York City.*

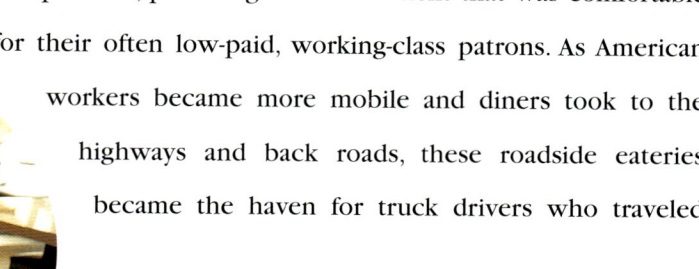

A neighborhood diner in Yeardon, Pennsylvania, serves as a local gathering spot for a group of friends.

"Rosie's is as simple as a hubcap and as unpretentious as its own rice pudding."

—Francis X. Clives

In this memorable image from the 1982 movie *Diner*, actors Kevin Bacon, Mickey Rourke, Daniel Stern, and Timothy Daly portray young men convening at the local diner to talk, joke, and hammer out their futures.

The diner crowd is anything but discriminating. College pals, families, travelers, old timers, truckers—even screaming babies—are all in a night's work at a twenty-four hour diner.

from coast to coast and often needed a quick, inexpensive meal at odd hours of the day and night.

The image of the diner as a roadside stop for burly truck drivers still looms large in American advertisements, building on the comparison to things that are "tough" or "rugged." The Bounty paper towel commercials selling "the quicker picker-upper" were classic diner imagery: a wise-cracking waitress, husky truck drivers at the counter, a no-nonsense approach, and a hard-working product to clean up the mess. An advertisement for heartburn relief also benefits from the diner image as a truck drivers' sanctuary: Where better than a diner, complete with artery-clogging delights such as chicken-fried steak, or bacon and eggs, to advertise the need for quick, inexpensive heartburn relief?

Rosie's Diner, of the Bounty commercials, is a 1946 Paramount Diner, and was relocated from New Jersey to Michigan in 1990. Its popularity as a classic image of a working-class diner is evidenced by its function as a backdrop to over a hundred other television advertisements.

TEENAGE RESTLESSNESS

The diner as a symbol of youth and restlessness is another popular image furthered by movies and television. *American Graffiti*, a 1973 movie directed by George Lucas, explores the unsettled lives of a group of teenagers on the brink of change in California: an all-American boy about to leave for college, his high-school sweetheart who wants him to stay, a high-school intellectual with doubts about his future, a "cool" older boy who drives fast and cruises Main Street, and a high-school "nerd" who wants to be cool. The film bombards us with images of their youthful exuberance—the 1932 Ford Deuce Coupe, the 1958 Impala, the pony-tailed, gum-chewing teenager, Wolfman Jack's nonstop disk-jockey show—and these images come together at the popular meeting place, Mel's Drive-In. The success of the film inspired the television show, *Happy Days*, which furthered the image of the local diner as a beloved, teenage hangout.

YOUTHFUL ANGST

Diner, a popular movie released in 1982, also revolves around a group of young men hanging out together, this time in an East Coast diner, in Baltimore. Writer/director Barry Levinson uses the image of the diner as a symbol of youthful angst, a time in one's life when friends are everything and the future is filled with doubt and indecision. These men are in their early twenties, they've known each other since high school, and though they're moving in different directions, they still converge at the local diner as often as possible to talk, joke, and figure out their futures. This film revels in the image of the diner as more atmosphere than food: It is the conversation, the comfortable environment, the convenience, and the comfort of friends which take center stage at this diner.

Actors Diane Ladd and Ellen Burstyn skill-fully portrayed unforgettable waitresses working at a scruffy diner in the 1975 film *Alice Doesn't Live Here Anymore*.

HOME AWAY FROM HOME

Another popular image of diners is cultivated in films such as *Alice Doesn't Live Here Anymore*, its television spin-off, *Alice*, and a recent television show, *Roseanne*. Two striking images which have found their way into the heart of American culture are the concept of the independent, self-reliant diner waitress, and the notion of the diner as a home away from home for people of all ages. In the film, Alice is a thirty-five-year-old single mother of a twelve-year-old son; after her truck driver husband is unexpectedly killed in a traffic accident, she sets off on an odyssey through the Southwest in pursuit of her dream of being a singer. Along the way she takes a job as a waitress in a diner, and it is there that she becomes good friends with a fellow waitress, falls in love with a divorced farmer, and begins to believe in herself as a strong, independent woman.

The diner in this film and in the subsequent television shows serves as a reveal-

THE QUEST FOR THE PERFECT BREAKFAST

Many folks grew up with diners and have always known them as places serving good, home-cooked meals in an inviting, friendly atmosphere. Others, however, who long associated diners with greasy hamburgers and lonely truck drivers, only found the charm of diners after their search for the perfect breakfast. Diner breakfasts are known for their twenty-four-hour availability, fresh, hot coffee, a multitude of filling, appetizing breakfast combinations, and a very reasonable price.

ABOVE
At the Munson Diner in New York City, a classic 1950s Kullman model, a family says grace before digging in.

Diner Slang

Diner lore has it that an informal vocabulary emerged over the years among diner waiters and waitresses as a way to speed up the processing of food. Servers would shout their order to the cooks behind the counters, who would begin whipping up an "Adam and Eve on a raft" while the server refilled a bottomless "cup of mud" for the regulars. While most diner regulars would agree that the majority of these phrases are rarely used, some diners have perpetuated these terms by printing them on their menus.

Adam and Eve on a raft: two scrambled eggs on toast
Beef Manhattan: roast beef sandwich on a hard roll, dipped in gravy
Birdseed: dry breakfast cereal
Black and tan: salt and pepper
Blond and sweet: coffee with sugar and cream
Bottomless cup of Joe: unlimited refills on coffee
Brownies: overcooked ends from the outside of leftover beef
A choke and puke: trucker lingo for roadside diners
Coffee and: coffee and a doughnut
Cup of mud: coffee
CB: cheeseburger
CJ: cream cheese and jelly
Dipped: a bun (hamburger, hot dog, or chili dog) that's dipped in gravy
Dog in a bun: hot dog
Dragged thru the garden: hot dog with gobs of mustard, onions, pickles, peppers, and tomatoes
Dressed: a sandwich with lettuce, tomatoes, onions, mayonnaise, and mustard
A grease spot: a hamburger
Fluff it: add whipped cream
Joe: coffee
Nervous pudding: Jello
PC: plain chocolate milk
PBJ: peanut butter and jelly sandwich
Raft: slice of toast
Red hots: spiced hot dogs
Sinker: doughnut
Squeeze one: pour a glass of orange juice
Twins: a pair of hot dogs on one plate
A velvet: a milkshake with milk, flavoring, and ice cream

ing backdrop to a host of adults who see the diner as their home away from home:
the regulars, the men and women who sidle up to the counter and claim their stool,
the folks who are handed coffee by the waitresses without the need for a spoken
exchange. The image of the diner as a community focal point, where conversation
mixes with the gossip of the day's events and the music from the jukebox, is an
image that has taken hold as an American institution. It is an image of the diner as
a place where the displaced, the traveler, the lonely, and the new in town can feel a
sense of belonging and recognition. It is a place where everyone can feel at home.

Linda Lavin, as Alice, serves up laughter and
heartburn to actors Martha Raye and Dave
Madden in the popular television show *Alice*.

Leo's Diner by Gordon Inyard.

Skip's Diner by Don Sawyer.

"... Then I'll take a chicken salad sandwich on toast. Now all you have to do is hold the chicken, bring me the toast, give me the check for the chicken salad sandwich, and you haven't broken any rules"

—Robert Dupea (played by Jack Nicholson), trying to order a simple piece of toast
from a waitress who will allow no substitutions, in the classic diner scene from *Five Easy Pieces*

BREAKFAST SPECIALS

All breakfasts served with unlimited coffee and choice of juice:

Buttermilk pancakes served with fresh fruit and real maple syrup

Two eggs any style served with bacon or sausage and toast

Blueberry pancakes, two eggs, side of bacon

Country-style omelet, English muffin, side of pancakes

Blueberry muffins, two eggs, sausage or bacon

Golden brown waffles served with fresh fruit and syrup

Thick French toast served with fresh strawberries

CLASSIC COOKING

The image of diners as home to tasty, satisfying food is occasionally marred by the inconsistencies inherent in thousands of privately-owned diners cooking individually prepared meals across the country. The fact that this image flourishes, however, is testament to the overwhelming agreement that diner food is the cornerstone of genuine, American home cooking. Whether it's roadhouse taverns serving skillet-cooked, country-fried steak, or classic diners serving baked chicken and rice, the foods dished out at diners across America symbolize an infatuation with the simple, basic meals of the past.

Classic diner food is unpretentious and simple; it combines strong, vibrant flavors, fresh ingredients, and personal, hands-on preparation. Although diner cooking has evolved over the years, with cooks having greater access to ethnic, exotic, and regional cuisines, as well as improved technology in the

Mouth-watering pies, waiting for a fluff of whipped cream, peer out enticingly from their glass enclosure.

kitchen, the time-honored diner menu is more likely to offer meatloaf and potatoes than hickory-smoked duck breast with raspberries; the desserts will be closer to apple pie and pineapple upside-down cake than cornmeal-anise pound cake served with spiced poached pears. Diner food is back-to-basics cooking; with its emphasis on simplicity and sincerity, diners have once again become American's most popular eating adventure.

THE DINER WAITRESS

"Have your orders ready, girls!" calls Elvira, the diner proprietor and waitress of *The Halfway Diner*, a short story by John Sayles. "Watcha need, hon," says the permed-haired, puckered-mouthed waitress in *Grub*, an essay by Scott Russell Sanders. "It's all good, same as every day," she says in response to his request as to what's good to eat. "She tugs a pencil from her perm, drums ringed fingers on the order pad . . . So what'll it be, sugar?"

The Diner Store

For diner aficionados, a visit to The Diner Store in Rockford, Michigan, presents a chance to see the artwork of owners and diner lovers Jerry and Madeline Berta. On display are their small ceramic sculptures of diners, neon sculptures, and other work, along with a bevy of coffee mugs, T-shirts, and Coca-Cola memorabilia. Jerry Berta bought a vacant 1947 O'Mahony diner in 1987, converted it to a studio and showroom, and moved it to its present location. It became such a popular attraction that in 1990 he bought Rosie's Diner, a 1946 Paramount, and moved it right next door to The Diner Store. Rosie's Diner served as backdrop to more than a hundred TV advertisements, and is well known as the home of "the quicker-picker-upper," Bounty paper towels.

The Diner Store, 4500 14 Mile Road, Rockford, Michigan (616) 866-2787.

The diner waitress—chatty, friendly, knows all the regulars by name—has become as much an American icon as the diner itself, a much loved symbol of the tough but kind, all-American working woman.

Prior to World War II, women were rarely seen on the working side of diners. Men owned, cooked, cleaned, and served customers and, until the 1930s, were the predominant customers in diners. When the war took away many of their employees, diners began recruiting women to work as food servers and handlers. The woman as diner waitress caught on, and today's diner waitresses often liken themselves to bartenders: listening to customers' problems, offering advice, watching over their customers with nurturing concern.

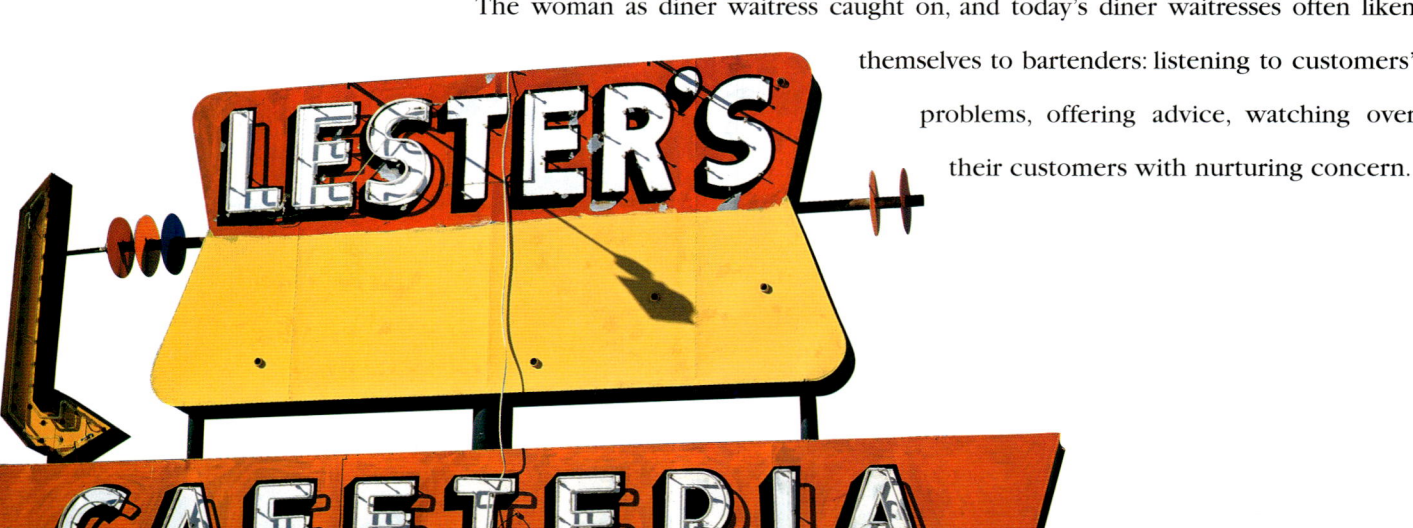

Valley Diner by Vincent Tango. College coeds converge upon the Valley Diner in this colorful depiction of a bustling East Coast eatery.

A short order cook flips sizzling burgers on a hot griddle.

For many, culinary heaven is defined by the consummate diner breakfast: crispy bacon, egg-battered French toast, and a generous side of hash browns. *Market Diner, New York City.*

Popular diner waitresses of American culture include television's Flo, the wise-cracking, "Kiss my grits" waitress from Mel's Diner; Alice, the single-mom waitress also of Mel's; Roseanne and her sister from the television show *Roseanne*; and Rosie, the hard-working, practical waitress of the Bounty paper towel advertisements. The mythic diner waitress, with her requisite tools of the trade—an order pad and a pen stuck behind her ear—knows when to fill your coffee, whether you take cream or sugar, and how you like your eggs.

DINER PATRONS: AN ECLECTIC GATHERING

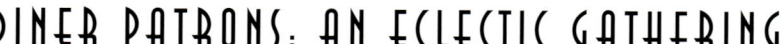

High-school pals, late-night revelers, families, travelers, old-timers, and truckers: The diner crowd is as complex as it is simple. What unites these diverse groups is their search for a cheap, bustling, dependable establishment where a good, home-cooked meal is almost always a sure thing, and the atmosphere is always welcoming.

AMERICAN DINERS ABROAD

American-style food and American-style decor is not just for Americans anymore: Lovers of American diners have transported the spirit of diners, if not the buildings themselves, overseas. Fatty Arbuckle, a notorious figure of the early Hollywood era, is being resurrected in the Fatty Arbuckle's American Diners proliferating throughout the United Kingdom. The restaurant chain created a theme diner based on American vintage movies, popular American music from the 1960s, and American-style food such as hamburgers, ribs, and potatoes, as well as pancakes, ice cream, and apple pie. Ed Debevic's, a caricature of a diner based upon a mythical diner owner, opened one of its chains in Japan. Themed diners, commemorating the youthfulness and energy associated with the diners of America's past, are fast becoming a part of America's depiction overseas.

Diners endure because they provide more than just food. Diners satisfy a longing for comfort and fun, for an opportunity to engage in unpretentious conversation, and for the chance to engage in simple pleasures such as an old song on a jukebox, a plate of hot french fries, or a black-and-white milkshake.

Although some have tried, diners can not be defined as one thing to everyone. Diners can be family gathering places, community kitchens, resting spots for weary motorists, greasy hamburger joints, or simply a local neighborhood restaurant in which to swap stories, catch up on gossip, or share idle chatter.

As icons from the past, diners have become a part of American culture that endures, as much for their diversity as for their ability to tap into a collective yearning for a return to simplicity and old-fashioned goodness. As restaurants of the present, diners survive because of a continuous need for friendly service, simple choices, and an informal atmosphere that any age group can enjoy. Some revere diners as places of beauty and authenticity; others are linked to diners for the imagined innocence of a past era. Still others appreciate diners for their regional specialties, while

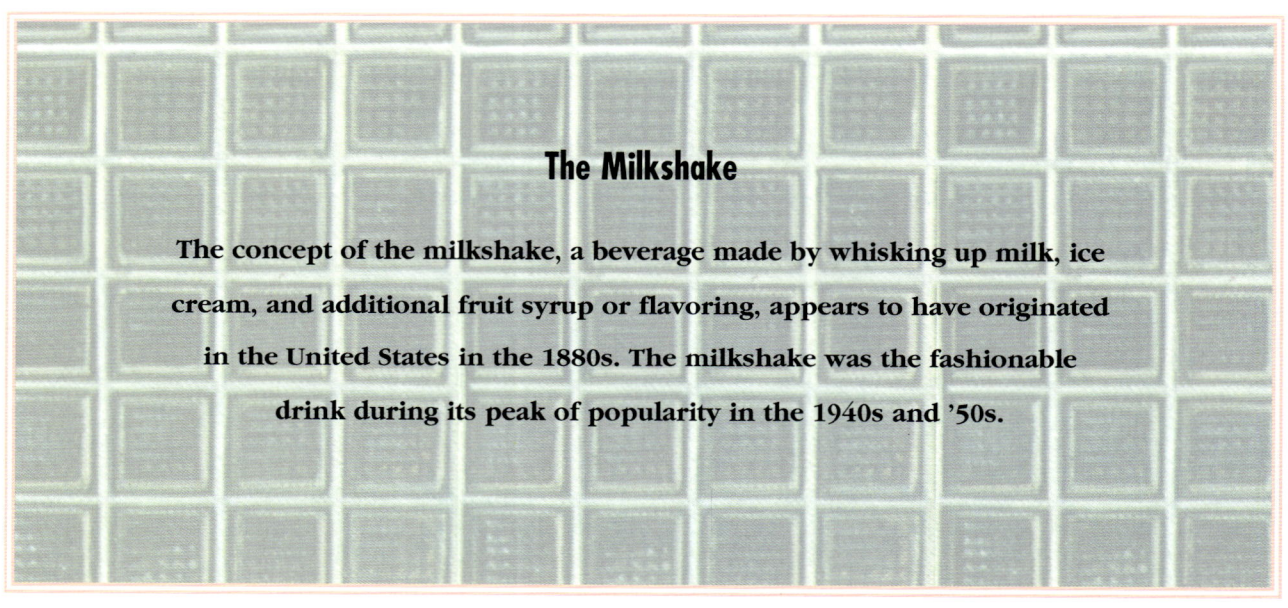

The Milkshake

The concept of the milkshake, a beverage made by whisking up milk, ice cream, and additional fruit syrup or flavoring, appears to have originated in the United States in the 1880s. The milkshake was the fashionable drink during its peak of popularity in the 1940s and '50s.

others enjoy their big breakfasts and blue plate specials. Perhaps what's most notable about America's popular cuisine, from East Coast to West, is how entertaining, how inviting, and, finally, how accessible it is, to all who seek its charms.

OPPOSITE
While many diner buffs count only prefabricated diners as "true" diners, the affable Blue Diner, with its opaque blue-glass exterior, is an example of a diner made on-site. The new model, its roof-topped coffee cup adding to its charm, replaced an old barrel-roofed model. *The Blue Diner, Boston, Massachusetts.*

BELOW
Diners endure because they provide everyone with the opportunity to engage in life's simpler pleasures—a wistful song on the jukebox, an onion-ring topped cheeseburger, or the purely decadent pleasure of a thick, strawberry shake.

> "... she called the Halfway the Halfway because everyplace on earth is halfway between somewhere and somewhere else."
>
> —John Sayles, *The Halfway Diner*

INDEX